NORDSTROM
FRIENDS AND FAMILY
COOKBOOK

Nordstrom Friends and Family Cookbook

HEARTWARMING RECIPES FOR YOUR TABLE

Executive Chef Michael Northern

with Diane Morgan

PHOTOGRAPHS BY E.J. ARMSTRONG

CHRONICLE BOOKS
SAN FRANCISCO

Text copyright © 2003 by Nordstrom, Inc.
Photographs copyright © 2003 by E.J. Armstrong.
All rights reserved. No part of this book may be reproduced in any form
without written permission from the publisher.

Library of Congress Cataloging-in-Publication Data:

Northern, Michael.
Nordstrom friends and family cookbook : heartwarming recipes for your table /
Michael Northern with Diane Morgan ; photographs by E.J. Armstrong.
    p. cm.
  ISBN 0-8118-3999-0 (Hardcover)
  1. Cookery. I. Morgan, Diane, 1955- II. Title.
  TX714.N674 2003
  641.5—dc21
                              2003003892

Manufactured in China.

Design and typesetting by Gretchen Scoble
Prop styling by Baroness Edna
Food styling by Patty Wittmann and Diana Isaiou

The photographer wishes to thank the entire team who worked on this project and the generous
support of Sara Schneider and Michael Northern, who brought the photography on this project to
the level we all had envisioned. And of course the never-ending support of the Antique liquidator
family, who constantly provided us with the perfect prop at a moment's notice.

10 9 8 7 6 5 4 3 2 1

Published exclusively for Nordstrom, Inc., by Chronicle Books LLC.

Chronicle Books LLC
85 Second Street
San Francisco, California 94105
www.chroniclebooks.com

To those who find comfort and joy in preparing great meals
for friends and family.

Contents

Preface

On behalf of everyone at Nordstrom, I am pleased to present *Nordstrom Friends and Family Cookbook.* It is a compendium of treasured recipes from the talented teams who work in our restaurants, as well as from other Nordstrom employees and friends. From the book's inception, our focus has been to offer a singular collection of dishes that can be easily cooked at home with wonderful results—recipes to enjoy and share with your friends and family.

Although we celebrated our one hundredth anniversary in business in 2001, food and restaurants are relatively new to Nordstrom. Our first restaurant, opened in 1973, was a small café in our flagship store in downtown Seattle. Since that time, it has been gratifying to see this humble early effort evolve into the unique and exciting restaurants that we now offer in many of our stores. Food has always been a special way for us to take care of our customers while they are shopping. Our restaurants enrich the customer experience at Nordstrom and provide the company with an element that sets us apart from the marketplace. The vitality and energy that our restaurants provide by offering a meeting place and sense of community have grown in importance to us and to our customers over the years.

At its heart, our business is about people. The thousands of employees that make up the Nordstrom team personify the goals and objectives our founder, John W. Nordstrom, set out for us in 1901. It is also about you, the customer, because without you our business would not exist. Food is a common bond that brings diverse people and cultures together.

This is our first cookbook, and we hope that you enjoy the recipes. It's been a fun and learning experience for us to work as a team to create this beautiful volume. Have fun in the kitchen, but most of all, share these recipes with family and friends.

—Blake Nordstrom
President

Introduction

Food has the power to transport us back to an earlier time and place and to connect us to memories and feelings as if we were still there. It is a natural link to our loved ones, enriching our experiences while providing us with nourishment. *Nordstrom Friends and Family Cookbook* explores the diversity of these experiences, as contributors share special recipes that connect them to moments of comfort, caring, and affection.

As I conceptualized this book, I was drawn back to a special time at my grandmother's farmhouse in Stevens Point, Wisconsin. Although thirty-five years have passed, my memory of a breakfast she prepared is more powerful now than ever. It was five in the morning and the woodstove was lit, burning hot with flames dancing about inside. A solitary lightbulb barely illuminated the kitchen—the depth and shadows of the room seemed painted with mystery. My grandmother prepared a breakfast of eggs snatched from beneath the chickens in the coops, cereal with fresh milk from the cows, home-smoked bacon cut as thick as you could cook it, and hot doughnuts bubbling cheerfully in a cast-iron skillet. Little did I know then of the power of the experience that she had created on that crisp early morning. I have traveled back to that special memory many times and have drawn great inspiration from that simple experience of food prepared with caring and love.

Including "friends and family" in the title of this book is a tip-off that there are not only recipes for entertaining but also for informal occasions where simplicity and comfort are key. Even in today's quick-paced world, where an over-abundance of food cooked faster than you can pay for it is the norm, there is a yearning for honest food cooked at home.

Foods cooked at home, whether simple or elaborate, are an opportunity to share a meal with people about whom we care. I once had the opportunity to travel in Italy for the pleasure of learning about the food and culture. Beyond the foods I discovered, I was most touched by the Italian sense of priorities, where friends and family are held first, food and cooking next, and the world of commerce in its place—last. The gathering of ingredients, the careful preparation of the meal, and the relaxed celebration with friends and family at the table is the grounding point for daily life. At home, there is no such thing as a bad meal—only good meals, great meals, and incredible meals. In selecting these recipes and the stories that accompany them, I had an overriding desire to express the pleasure that comes from sharing meals with friends and family.

Nordstrom has long owned and operated restaurants and espresso bars within its many stores. Over time, the restaurants have evolved to feature a diverse array of concepts. The restaurant division includes the Classic Cafe; the interactive and visual Marketplace Cafe; Cafe Bistro, with its exhibition kitchen; and the traditional Nordstrom Grill. Espresso venues greet the customers when they enter the stores and include our traditional Espresso Bar, the contemporary Ebar, and the colorful and interactive In House Cafe and Coffee Bar. These restaurants and espresso operations provide our stores with a sense of community and place while enriching the shopping experience. Moreover, a commitment to customer service and the belief in serving quality food have helped elevate the popularity of all of these restaurants.

As these different venues become more popular, and as our dedication to becoming better at what we do each day keeps us energized, we find ourselves continually asked by our customers for our recipes. What better way to satisfy these requests and provide exceptional service than to assemble a book of favorites!

Early on, I knew that I did not want to create this book as a marketing piece for the Nordstrom Restaurant Division. Instead, I felt that the recipes should be a selection of the best of what I could gather from Nordstrom's forty thousand employees. With this in mind, I set about collecting favorite recipes from Nordstrom chefs, other Nordstrom employees, and the Nordstrom family. From this pool of offerings I chose those that best complemented the intended fabric of the book. These recipes are presented here, alongside popular Nordstrom menu items and dishes that I have been fortunate enough to learn from fellow chefs during my thirty-year career. The determining factors for selection were quality, taste, and the ability to be prepared in the average home.

Nordstrom Friends and Family Cookbook is ultimately about the pleasure that the great and memorable meals in our lives provide, and the role that food plays in bringing us closer to our friends and family. The wide range of tempting recipes speaks to the realities of preparing food at home, while exploring new and exciting flavors. Many of the dishes celebrate and complement the seasons of the year, heartwarming and nourishing during the cooler winter months and vibrant and colorful during the warm days of spring and summer. The book is organized to make it easy for you to create a menu from the various sections. You will find dozens of wonderful possibilities by simply following your instincts. Try pairing the formal with the rustic, offer a starter or salad alongside a selection from the grill, or choose a dish that you can make in advance to go along with one that must be prepared at the last minute.

Our hope is that the dishes you try inspire you and that they join the fabric of your life, becoming a part of your special celebrations, seasons, holidays, and casual gatherings of friends and family. Then do as we have done—pass them along to those whom you love and cherish.

—MICHAEL NORTHERN

o ROASTED GARLIC WITH WARM CRUSTY BAGUETTES 14

o BRUSCHETTA WITH TOMATO-BASIL TOPPING 16

o CILANTRO-LIME DIP 17

o BISTRO FRENCH FRIES WITH KALAMATA OLIVE AIOLI DIP 18

o PRINCE EDWARD ISLAND STEAMED MUSSELS 21

o GINGER-SESAME-MARINATED ASPARAGUS 22

o FRESH MOZZARELLA CAPRESE 23

o SUMMER CORN SALAD WITH CHAMPAGNE VINAIGRETTE AND PLUM TOMATOES 24

o COLESLAW WITH APPLE AND FENNEL 26

o CHAMPAGNE AND GORGONZOLA POTATO SALAD 27

o GRILLED VEGETABLE SALAD 29

STARTERS & SALADS

o MAYTAG BLUE CHEESE AND PEAR SALAD 31

o WARM GOAT CHEESE AND SPINACH SALAD 32

o SUMMER FRUIT SALAD WITH CANDIED CASHEWS 35

o BLACKENED SALMON CAESAR 36

o CHINESE CHICKEN SALAD 38

o PESTO CHICKEN SALAD 41

Roasted Garlic
with Warm Crusty Baguettes ⇢ serves 6 to 8

When a basic technique, namely roasting, is applied to a simple ingredient, such as garlic, big flavors emerge that turn the humble bulb into a showcase appetizer. When I first developed this recipe for a restaurant, we decided to offer it as a complimentary appetizer. Roasted garlic soon became the most requested recipe at the restaurant.

Rather than the overpowering, pungent taste of raw garlic, roasted garlic adds a rustic, earthy flavor to sauces, salad dressings, and casseroles. Given how easy roasted garlic is to make and, as you'll see, how often it is used in recipes throughout the book, I suggest roasting extra heads to have on hand.

4 large heads garlic

1 tablespoon extra-virgin olive oil

Kosher salt

Freshly ground black pepper

2 baguettes, warmed

$^1/_2$ cup (1 stick) unsalted butter,
    at room temperature

Preheat the oven to 375°F. Trim any stray roots from the bottom of the garlic heads, then carefully cut a slice off of the top of each head to expose the cloves. Rub the trimmed garlic heads with the olive oil and a sprinkling of salt and pepper.

Place the prepared garlic in a small baking dish. Pour in hot water to reach one third of the way up the sides of the garlic heads. Cover the dish with aluminum foil, crimping the edges to seal securely. Bake the garlic until lightly browned, soft, and tender (you'll be able to pierce it easily with a paring knife), 1$^1/_2$ to 2 hours (depending on the size of the bulbs). Remove from the oven, drain any remaining water, and let cool slightly.

Serve the roasted garlic warm with the baguettes and with butter packed into a small ramekin. For guests unfamiliar with eating roasted garlic, be a great host and demonstrate how to break the heads apart and squeeze the garlic pulp from its papery sheaths.

COOK'S NOTE: *If you roast extra heads of garlic, refrigerate the roasted garlic in a covered container for up to 1 week. When a recipe calls for roasted garlic, simply break apart the heads and squeeze the garlic pulp out of their skins.*

Bruschetta
with Tomato-Basil Topping ↔ serves 4

The word bruschetta *is from the Italian* bruscare, *meaning "to roast over coals." As with all Italian cooking, the quality of a dish lies in the details—applying simple techniques and using the freshest ingredients. Bruschetta is a perfect example. Start with a coarse, crusty artisanal bread, buy the best extra-virgin olive oil you can afford, and only use vine-ripened tomatoes at the peak of the summer growing season. At home, I make this dish with tomatoes ripe from the garden and still warm from the sun. My wife, a dedicated gardener and New Jersey native, knows her tomatoes. We love eating this while sitting on the deck with friends as the sun sets on a long, hot August day.*

TOMATO-BASIL TOPPING

1 pound vine-ripened tomatoes, cored, seeded,
    and diced

2 tablespoons chopped fresh basil

3 tablespoons extra-virgin olive oil

1 tablespoon balsamic vinegar

Kosher salt

Freshly ground black pepper

4 slices rustic bread, cut 3/4 inch thick from
    a round loaf

Extra-virgin olive oil for brushing

1 clove garlic, halved

Kosher salt

To make the Tomato-Basil Topping, in a bowl, combine the tomatoes, basil, olive oil, and balsamic vinegar and toss together. Season to taste with salt and pepper. Set aside at room temperature until ready to serve.

Allow the bread slices to dry slightly while preheating the broiler. If broiling, adjust the rack so that it is about 4 inches from the heat source. If grilling, preheat a gas grill to medium, or prepare a charcoal fire and wait until the coals reach the white ash stage and the fire begins to die down to low coals.

Brush both sides of the bread slices with olive oil. Rub one or both sides of each slice with the garlic, rubbing hard if you like a pronounced garlic taste, or gently if you prefer a milder flavor. Season the bread with a sprinkle of salt.

Broil or grill the bread until nicely browned on both sides, being careful not to burn it. Spoon some of the tomato-basil topping over each slice. Serve immediately.

Cilantro-Lime Dip

↔ serves 8

Big hits of fresh cilantro with bright undertones of citrus are the key players in this healthful and tasty bean dip. Create a fiesta-party feel when you serve this dip with a fresh salsa, a big bowl of tortilla chips, and a platter of crudités. Perfect for a crowd, this dip also works as a sandwich spread to layer with thinly sliced vegetables, grilled or raw, or something as simple as cucumber and sprouts. —ALICE AND RUSSELL DORR

1 cup packed cilantro leaves and tender stems

1 clove garlic

2 tablespoons coarsely chopped red onion

2 cans (15 ounces each) cannellini beans,
    drained and rinsed

2 tablespoons extra-virgin olive oil

2 tablespoons fresh lime juice

1 tablespoon fresh lemon juice

1/4 cup milk

1/2 teaspoon kosher salt

1/2 teaspoon freshly ground black pepper

3 plum tomatoes, cored, seeded, and diced

1 bag (20 ounces) tortilla chips

In a food processor fitted with the metal blade or in a blender, process the cilantro, garlic, and onion until finely minced. Add the cannellini beans, olive oil, lime juice, lemon juice, milk, salt, and pepper and process until a smooth purée forms. Transfer to a serving bowl, stir in the tomatoes, and then taste and adjust the seasoning. Cover and refrigerate for up to 8 hours before serving.

Remove the dip from the refrigerator 20 minutes before serving. Accompany with the tortilla chips.

Bistro French Fries
with Kalamata Olive Aioli Dip   ⇸ serves 6 to 8

At Cafe Bistro we have mastered the art of making great french fries. The secret lies in taking a few extra, easy steps: using the best Idaho potatoes available, cooking the fries twice to guarantee proper crispness, flavoring them with a fresh herb toss, and serving them with a surprising and delicious aioli dip laced with olives.

KALAMATA OLIVE AIOLI DIP

1 clove garlic

$1/2$ cup kalamata olives, pitted

2 tablespoons roasted garlic (page 14)

2 cups mayonnaise

2 tablespoons fresh lemon juice

BISTRO FRENCH FRIES

About 6 cups canola oil for deep-frying

Ice water

4 to 6 large Idaho potatoes, unpeeled and
well scrubbed

BISTRO FRENCH-FRY HERBS

1 teaspoon chopped fresh rosemary

1 teaspoon chopped fresh thyme

1 teaspoon chopped fresh flat-leaf parsley

1 teaspoon chopped fresh chives

Kosher salt

Freshly ground black pepper

To make the dip, in a food processor fitted with the metal blade, process the garlic, olives, and roasted garlic and pulse until finely chopped. Add the mayonnaise and lemon juice and process until the mixture is well blended and light purple. Transfer to a serving dish, cover, and refrigerate.

To make the fries, pour the oil to a depth of at least 3 inches in a large, deep saucepan. Heat the oil to 300°F. Have ready a rimmed baking sheet covered with a double thickness of paper towels.

While the oil is heating, fill a large bowl with ice water. Cut the potatoes lengthwise into strips about $3/8$ inch wide and place them into the ice water to prevent discoloring. When the oil is hot, drain the potatoes and dry them well.

Add the potatoes to the hot oil in small batches and fry until they float and begin to turn a pale gold, 10 to 12 minutes per batch. Using a slotted utensil, transfer the potatoes to the prepared baking sheet to drain. Skim the oil, removing small particles of potato, and set aside until ready to reheat.

Prepare the herbs. In a small bowl, stir together the rosemary, thyme, parsley, and chives.

About 15 minutes before serving, reheat the oil to 375°F. In small batches, fry the potatoes until they are light brown and crisp, 4 to 5 minutes per batch. Remove from the oil, drain on paper towels, and place in a bowl. Toss with the herb mixture. Season with salt and pepper. Serve immediately with the Kalamata Olive Aioli Dip.

Prince Edward Island Steamed Mussels ⇝ serves 4

Archaeologists have discovered that mussels have been used for food for over twenty thousand years. Too bad those early foragers didn't have this recipe! Packed with garlic, heated up with red pepper flakes, and swimming in a buttery wine sauce, this mussel recipe is a favorite at the Nordstrom Cafe Bistro.

At Cafe Bistro we like to use Prince Edward Island mussels because they are farm-raised in Canada on suspended ropes, which keep them off the silty sea bottom. As a result, the mussels are cleaner, sweeter, and more tender than other varieties. Whether Prince Edward Island or not, buy mussels with tightly closed shells or with shells that snap shut when tapped. Look for small to medium-sized mussels with a blue-black exterior. Discard any with broken shells. Serve these mussels with warm crusty bread as the start to a great meal.

2 tablespoons extra-virgin olive oil

3 shallots, minced

4 cloves garlic, minced

1/2 teaspoon red pepper flakes

2 pounds Prince Edward Island mussels

1/2 cup dry white wine

1/2 cup bottled clam juice

Kosher salt

Freshly ground black pepper

3 tablespoons unsalted butter

1/4 cup Gazpacho Salsa (page 107), or 1 large
    vine-ripened tomato, cored, seeded, and diced
    (see Cook's Note)

2 tablespoons chopped fresh flat-leaf parsley

In a large skillet over medium-high heat, warm the olive oil. Add the shallots, garlic, and red pepper flakes and sauté, stirring, until the garlic turns light tan, about 1 minute. Add the mussels, raise the heat to high, cover the skillet with a tight-fitting lid, and cook until the mussels begin to open, about 2 minutes. Add the white wine and simmer, uncovered, until fully reduced, 1 to 2 minutes. Reduce the heat to medium and add the clam juice, swirling the mussels to coat. Season generously with salt and pepper. Now, constantly swirling the mussels, add the butter and allow it to incorporate, then add the Gazpacho Salsa and the parsley, stir to coat well, and heat through.

Remove the mussels from the heat. Using tongs or a slotted spoon, transfer the mussels to a warmed serving bowl, discarding any that failed to open. Pour the pan sauce over the top. Serve immediately.

Cook's Note: *Although this recipe only calls for a small amount of Gazpacho Salsa, and a substitute is provided, I highly recommend taking the time to make a batch of the salsa. It has big, bold flavors that perfectly complement the mussels. With the balance of the salsa on hand, making the Grilled Salmon with Gazpacho Salsa (page 107) is a snap.*

Ginger-Sesame-Marinated Asparagus

↦ serves 6

Make this salad in the spring at the height of asparagus season, when markets display bundles of asparagus standing upright and orderly like soldiers on parade. Big fat spears work best for this salad, because they look great on a platter, and their meatiness absorbs the bright flavors of the dressing.

2 pounds jumbo asparagus

2 teaspoons kosher salt

Ice water

GINGER-SESAME DRESSING

1 cup canola oil

3 tablespoons Asian sesame oil

1/2 cup rice wine vinegar

1/2 cup sugar

1/4 cup soy sauce

1 1/2 teaspoons ground ginger

1 1/2 teaspoons dry mustard

1 teaspoon freshly ground black pepper

2 tablespoons sesame seeds, toasted
   (see Cook's Note, page 190)

Select a pan large enough to accommodate the asparagus when lying flat. Fill the pan two-thirds full with water. Cover and bring to a boil.

Snap off the woody bottom end of each asparagus spear then trim any ragged edges, or trim all the spears to a uniform length. Using a vegetable peeler, lightly peel the bottom half of each spear, removing only the thin, fibrous outer layer.

When the water boils, add the salt, and then add the asparagus. Cook the spears, uncovered, until they are bright green and crisp-tender without tasting raw, 5 to 6 minutes. To test for doneness, insert a paring knife into the thickest part of a spear—or, easier still, taste one.

Use tongs to remove the asparagus spears, placing them immediately in a large bowl of ice water. Cool for 1 to 2 minutes, and then drain and pat dry with paper towels. Place the cooled asparagus in a gallon-sized lock-top plastic bag. Set aside.

To make the Ginger-Sesame Dressing, in a small bowl, whisk together the canola oil, sesame oil, vinegar, sugar, soy sauce, ginger, mustard, and pepper until thoroughly blended.

Pour 3/4 cup of the dressing over the spears. Seal the bag, and then place in the refrigerator to chill and marinate for at least 1 hour. Pour the remaining dressing into a jar with a tight-fitting lid and reserve in the refrigerator for another use. It will keep for up to 1 month.

When ready to serve, arrange the asparagus spears on a serving platter and sprinkle with the toasted sesame seeds.

Fresh Mozzarella Caprese

↔ serves 6 to 8

As with many Italian dishes, this salad teaches the importance of simplicity through the use of a few specially chosen ingredients. Fresh mozzarella, with its silky texture and perfectly neutral flavor, seems destined for pairing with vine-ripened tomatoes and fragrant fresh basil. The unique twist here is a balsamic vinegar reduction that intensifies and mellows the flavor of the famed Italian vinegar. The salad, except for the dressing, can be assembled in advance and should be served at room temperature, making it a perfect choice for a picnic or potluck. —MICHAEL THOMS

1 cup balsamic vinegar

2 tablespoons sugar

Kosher salt

1 cup firmly packed arugula leaves, stems removed

4 large, vine-ripened tomatoes, preferably a mixture of colors, cored and sliced $1/4$ inch thick

Freshly ground black pepper

1 pound fresh mozzarella cheese, drained and sliced $1/4$ inch thick

20 fresh basil leaves

$1/4$ cup extra-virgin olive oil

Prepare a balsamic vinegar glaze by combining the vinegar, sugar, and a dash of salt in a small saucepan. Bring to a simmer over medium heat and cook until reduced by three fourths. Set aside and let cool to room temperature. If the glaze becomes too thick as it cools, stir in a few drops of water. It should be the consistency of chocolate syrup.

Meanwhile, scatter the arugula around a large serving platter. Arrange the tomatoes on the arugula. Season the tomato slices with salt and pepper. Top each tomato slice with a slice of mozzarella, and then top the cheese with a basil leaf.

When ready to serve, streak the salad first with the olive oil and then drizzle with the balsamic vinegar glaze.

Summer Corn Salad
with Champagne Vinaigrette and Plum Tomatoes ↬ serves 6 to 8

During the summer, when the markets are full of fresh-picked corn and true vine-ripened tomatoes, I use them as much as I can in salads, side dishes, and chowders. For this salad, buy either white or yellow corn—whichever is freshest—and use it right away, before its natural sugars turn to starch. You can grill the corn if you have the coals going, or you can simply boil it. If it is just picked, it will take only a few minutes by either method. Make the salad an hour or so before serving so the flavors have a chance to blend.

CHAMPAGNE VINAIGRETTE

1 shallot, quartered

1 small clove garlic

1 tablespoon Dijon mustard

2 tablespoons sugar

$1/8$ teaspoon kosher salt

Dash of freshly ground white pepper

$1/2$ cup Champagne vinegar

$1^1/2$ cups canola oil

3 ears corn, shucked and grilled or boiled

6 plum tomatoes, cored and cut into large chunks

1 shallot, minced

2 teaspoons chopped fresh tarragon

1 tablespoon chopped fresh flat-leaf parsley

$1^1/2$ cups firmly packed arugula leaves,
    stems removed

Kosher salt

Freshly ground black pepper

To make the Champagne Vinaigrette, in a blender or in a food processor fitted with the metal blade, process the shallot and garlic until finely minced. Add the mustard, sugar, salt, pepper, and vinegar. Process to combine the ingredients thoroughly. With the machine running, gradually add the oil in a thin, steady stream to form an emulsion. Taste and adjust the seasoning.

To prepare the salad, cut off the corn kernels from the cobs: working with 1 ear at a time, stand it upright, stem-end down, on a cutting board. Using a sharp knife, cut downward along the cob, removing the kernels and rotating the cob a quarter turn after each cut. Discard the cobs and scoop the kernels into a large bowl. You should have about 2 cups.

Add the tomatoes, shallot, tarragon, parsley, arugula, and $1/2$ cup of the Champagne Vinaigrette to the corn and stir to combine. Season to taste with salt and pepper. Let the salad sit at room temperature for about 1 hour before serving.

COOK'S NOTE: *Pour the remaining Champagne Vinaigrette into a bottle with a tight-fitting lid and store in the refrigerator for up to 1 month. This salad dressing is perfect for almost any mixed green or vegetable salad.*

Coleslaw with Apple and Fennel

↔ serves 8 to 10

Forget the usual shredded cabbage and carrot coleslaw served at summer barbecues. This slaw features sweet crisp apples, anise-flavored fennel, and a hint of tarragon along with the carrots and cabbage. Because the flavors need time to develop and blend, this is an ideal salad to make ahead for family gatherings, barbecues, and picnics. Experiment in the kitchen with other slaw variations, such as substituting jicama for the fennel and adding some cilantro, or using celery along with the apple and replacing the tarragon with celery seeds. —CHEF DAVID SHAW

6 cups shredded green cabbage

2 cups thinly sliced fennel (about 1 medium bulb),
    plus 1 tablespoon chopped fennel fronds

2 carrots, peeled and julienned

2 large Granny Smith apples, cored and julienned

3 tablespoons cider vinegar

2 tablespoons fresh lemon juice

2 tablespoons sugar

1$^1/_2$ cups mayonnaise

Kosher salt

Freshly ground black pepper

2 tablespoons fresh tarragon leaves

In a large bowl, toss together the cabbage, the fennel and fennel fronds, and the carrots. In another bowl, toss the apple with the cider vinegar and lemon juice until evenly coated, then add the apple to the cabbage mixture. Sprinkle the cabbage mixture with the sugar, add the mayonnaise, and then toss together until all the ingredients are well coated. Season to taste with salt and pepper, and toss again.

Transfer the salad to a serving bowl, scatter the tarragon leaves over the top, cover, and refrigerate until ready to serve. Make the salad 1 to 2 hours before serving so the flavors have time to develop.

Champagne and Gorgonzola Potato Salad ↔ serves 8 to 10

Unlike the traditional potato salads served at most summer barbecues, this one combines Champagne—yes, Champagne—with the wonderfully rich and earthy flavors of Gorgonzola cheese. Place this salad alongside a roasted pork tenderloin on a buffet table, or put it on your New Year's Eve menu to accompany a garlic-and-salt-crusted prime rib. —JOSEPH BOUNDS

$2^1/_2$ pounds small red potatoes

1 tablespoon kosher salt, plus salt to taste

$^1/_2$ cup Champagne

Freshly ground black pepper

$^1/_2$ cup mayonnaise

$^1/_2$ cup sour cream

$1^1/_2$ tablespoons Dijon mustard

$1^1/_2$ tablespoons cider vinegar

$1^1/_2$ cups (6 ounces) crumbled Gorgonzola cheese

2 celery stalks, chopped

3 green onions, including green tops,
    finely chopped

Place the potatoes in a 3- to 4-quart saucepan and cover with cold water. Bring to a boil over medium-high heat, add the 1 tablespoon salt, reduce the heat to medium, and simmer the potatoes, uncovered, until they are tender but not mushy when pierced with a knife, about 15 minutes. (For this recipe you want the potatoes to be tender but still firm.) Drain the potatoes in a colander, arrange them in a single layer on a rimmed baking sheet, and let cool to room temperature.

Cut the cooled potatoes into bite-sized pieces. Transfer them to a large bowl and pour the Champagne over them. Season to taste with salt and pepper, and then toss to combine. Let stand until the potatoes absorb the Champagne.

Meanwhile, in a mixing bowl, stir together the mayonnaise, sour cream, mustard, vinegar, Gorgonzola, celery, and green onions. Add the mayonnaise mixture to the potatoes and stir until the potatoes are evenly coated.

Transfer the salad to a serving bowl. Let it sit at room temperature for about 30 minutes before serving to allow the flavors to meld.

Grilled Vegetable Salad

↔ serves 6 as a main course

There are ho–hum grilled vegetable salads and then there are really great grilled vegetable salads. Just ask director Steven Spielberg. Once, while working for him, I made a grilled vegetable salad that he only gave a B rating. He was looking for a star–studded cast of vegetables. This is the recipe, and it earned a stellar review from the director.

1 pound jumbo asparagus

2 zucchini, cut lengthwise into $^1/_2$-inch-thick slices

3 ears corn, shucked

1 bunch green onions, root ends trimmed

2 tablespoons extra-virgin olive oil

Kosher salt

Freshly ground black pepper

2 avocados, halved, pitted, and diced

4 plum tomatoes, cored and cut into large chunks

2 bunches watercress, tough stems removes

10 ounces mixed baby greens

$^3/_4$ cup Sun-Dried Tomato Vinaigrette (page 32)

$^1/_2$ cup (2 ounces) freshly grated Parmesan cheese, preferably Parmigiano-Reggiano

1 lemon, cut into 6 wedges

1 lime, cut into 6 wedges

6 fresh dill sprigs

Prepare a medium fire in a charcoal grill, or preheat a gas grill on medium.

Snap off the woody bottom end of each asparagus spear, then trim away jagged edges, or trim all the spears to uniform lengths. Using a vegetable peeler, lightly peel off the bottom half of each spear, removing only the thin, fibrous outer layer. Lay the asparagus, zucchini, corn, and green onions on rimmed baking sheets. Brush on both sides with olive oil and season with salt and pepper.

Place the vegetables in a single layer directly over the fire. Grill, turning as needed to prevent burning. The vegetables are done when the zucchini is nicely browned, the corn is speckled mahogany with a touch of char, and the onions and asparagus are striped with dark grill marks. Remove from the grill and let cool slightly.

Working with 1 corn ear at a time, stand it upright, stem-end down, on a cutting board. Using a sharp knife, cut downward along the cob, removing the kernels and rotating the cob a quarter turn after each cut. Discard the cobs and scoop the kernels into a large bowl.

Cut the zucchini slices into bite-sized triangles. Slice the asparagus on an angle into 1-inch lengths. Chop the green onions. Toss the grilled vegetables with the avocados, tomatoes, watercress, mixed baby greens, and the vinaigrette. Season to taste with salt and pepper. Transfer the salad to individual salad plates. Sprinkle each serving with some of the cheese, and garnish with a wedge each of lemon and lime and a dill sprig. Serve immediately.

Maytag Blue Cheese and Pear Salad

↔ serves 6 as a main course

Maytag, a creamy and full-flavored blue cheese, is produced in limited quantities in Newton, Iowa, by a group of dedicated cheese makers. Although this artisanal cheese served as inspiration for this salad, other blue cheeses can be substituted. Along with using terrific cheese, select ripe, yet firm, juicy-sweet pears such as Bosc or Anjou. The Champagne Vinaigrette recipe used for this salad marries the flavors without overpowering the dish. It's a versatile dressing to have on your pantry shelf. —FARIS ZOMA

CANDIED WALNUTS

Vegetable-oil cooking spray

1 large egg white

10 ounces walnut halves and pieces

    (about 2^1/$_2$ cups)

^{3}/$_4$ cup firmly packed light brown sugar

1 head romaine lettuce, trimmed and torn into

    bite-sized pieces

10 ounces mixed baby greens

2 ripe Bosc or Anjou pears, cored

    and cut into ^{3}/$_4$-inch dice

1 red bell pepper, seeded, deribbed, and julienned

2 cups (^{1}/$_2$ pound) crumbled Maytag blue cheese

^{3}/$_4$ cup Champagne Vinaigrette (page 24), or more

    as needed

Kosher salt

Freshly ground black pepper

To make the Candied Walnuts, preheat the oven to 325°F. Spray the bottom of a rimmed baking sheet with the cooking spray. In a bowl, whisk the egg white until it is completely foamy and no liquid remains. Fold in the walnuts and brown sugar. Toss gently to coat. Arrange the walnuts on the prepared baking sheet, keeping the individual pieces separate. Bake until the egg white–sugar mixture is cooked through and the nuts are golden brown, 12 to 14 minutes. Loosen the nuts from the pan with a spatula. Set aside on a plate to cool.

To assemble the salad, in a large bowl, combine the romaine, mixed baby greens, pears, bell pepper, cheese, and the walnuts. Add the ^{3}/$_4$ cup Champagne Vinaigrette and toss gently to coat the ingredients evenly. Add more dressing if needed. Season to taste with salt and pepper. As you toss the salad, the heavier ingredients will fall to the bottom. This is good.

Using tongs, transfer the salad to large, chilled salad bowls or plates (see Cook's Note), building height in the center. Evenly distribute the heavier ingredients remaining at the bottom of the bowl on top of each salad.

COOK'S NOTE: *A chilled salad bowl or plate makes a big difference, keeping the salad cool and crisp. Simply pop a few into the freezer, or refrigerator before beginning.*

Warm Goat Cheese and Spinach Salad

↔ serves 4

The tangy and rich taste of goat cheese turns up twice here: once in the dressing and then in a shower of crumbled bits over the greens. The deep, earthy taste of spinach partners with the sharp notes and visual appeal of baby endive and is accented with croutons and the sweet sensations produced by oven–dried plum tomatoes.

OVEN-DRIED TOMATOES

8 plum tomatoes, cored and halved

1 tablespoon balsamic vinegar

1 tablespoon extra-virgin olive oil

Kosher salt

Freshly ground black pepper

1 tablespoon chopped fresh rosemary

SUN-DRIED TOMATO VINAIGRETTE

1/2 cup (about 2 ounces) dry-packed
    sun-dried tomatoes

Boiling water

2/3 cup balsamic vinegar

1 1/3 cups extra-virgin olive oil

1 teaspoon kosher salt

1/2 teaspoon freshly ground black pepper

6 tablespoons chopped fresh basil

To make the Oven-Dried Tomatoes, preheat the oven to 250°F. In a bowl, gently toss the tomato halves with the vinegar and olive oil until evenly coated. Set a cooling rack on a rimmed baking sheet and arrange the tomato halves, cut-sides up, on the rack. Season the tomatoes with a sprinkling of salt, pepper, and rosemary. Bake the tomatoes until they are about half their original size and the flavors are deeply concentrated, 2 1/2 to 3 hours. Rotate the pan 180 degrees about halfway through the roasting time to ensure even cooking. Set aside and let cool to room temperature.

To make the Sun-Dried Tomato Vinaigrette, in a heatproof bowl, soak the sun-dried tomatoes in boiling water to cover until softened, about 10 minutes. Drain the tomatoes. In a blender or in a food processor fitted with the metal blade, combine the softened tomatoes, vinegar, and olive oil and process until the tomatoes are puréed and the mixture is well blended. Season with the salt and pepper. Add the basil and pulse for a few seconds. Set aside.

continued

WARM GOAT CHEESE DRESSING

1 cup heavy (whipping) cream

3 ounces fresh goat cheese

2 tablespoons red wine vinegar

$1/4$ teaspoon kosher salt

$1/8$ teaspoon freshly ground white pepper

1 tablespoon chopped fresh basil

1 pound baby spinach

1 head (about 2 ounces) baby frisée,
    torn into bite-sized pieces

$1^{1}/_{2}$ cups homemade or store-bought croutons

1 cup ($1/4$ pound) crumbled fresh goat cheese

Kosher salt

Freshly ground black pepper

To make the Warm Goat Cheese Dressing, in a small saucepan over low heat, whisk together the cream, goat cheese, vinegar, salt, and pepper. Continue to whisk until the dressing is warm and reduced in volume by half. Remove from the heat and stir in the basil. Keep warm for up to 1 hour, or cover, refrigerate, and rewarm when ready to serve.

To assemble the salad, in a large bowl, combine the spinach, frisée, croutons, and half of the crumbled goat cheese. Drizzle with $3/4$ cup of the tomato vinaigrette and toss until evenly coated. Season to taste with salt and pepper.

Divide the salad among chilled bowls, building height in the center. Garnish each salad with 4 oven-dried tomato halves. Scatter the remaining crumbled goat cheese on the top, dividing it evenly. Complete each salad by drizzling about 3 tablespoons of the Warm Goat Cheese Dressing over the top.

Cook's Note: *The Sun-Dried Tomato Vinaigrette recipe yields 2 cups dressing, although you'll only need ¾ cup for this salad. This is a bonus! Place the extra dressing in a tightly sealed jar and refrigerate for up to 2 weeks. Use it on other salads, or spoon it over Italian Grilled Vegetables (page 93) just before serving.*

Summer Fruit Salad with Candied Cashews ↦ serves 6 to 8

Take advantage of fresh cherries during their brief but delicious appearance at the beginning of summer. Tossed in salads, packed in pie crusts, or spooned over ice cream, cherries star beautifully in both sweet and savory dishes. Here, salad greens mixed with cherries, peach slices, and sweet, crunchy cashews are drizzled with a cherry-rich balsamic vinaigrette.

CANDIED CASHEWS

Vegetable-oil cooking spray

1 large egg white

10 ounces whole cashews (about 2$^{1}/_{2}$ cups)

$^{3}/_{4}$ cup firmly packed light brown sugar

DARK CHERRY BALSAMIC VINAIGRETTE

$^{1}/_{2}$ cup balsamic vinegar

$^{1}/_{4}$ cup sugar

1 tablespoon minced roasted garlic (page 14)

$^{1}/_{2}$ cup cherry preserves

$^{1}/_{4}$ cup red wine vinegar

1 cup canola oil

Kosher salt

Freshly ground black pepper

1 pound mixed baby greens

$^{3}/_{4}$ pound fresh cherries, pitted and halved

3 ripe peaches, halved, pitted, and thinly sliced

Kosher salt

Freshly ground black pepper

To make the Candied Cashews, preheat the oven to 325°F. Spray the bottom of a rimmed baking sheet with the cooking spray. In a bowl, whisk the egg white until it is completely foamy and no liquid remains. Fold in the cashews and brown sugar. Toss gently to coat. Arrange the cashews on the prepared baking sheet, keeping the individual pieces separate. Bake until the egg white–sugar mixture is cooked through and the nuts are golden brown, 12 to 14 minutes. Loosen the nuts from the pan with a spatula. Set aside on a plate to cool.

To make the Dark Cherry Balsamic Vinaigrette, in a small saucepan over medium heat, bring the balsamic vinegar and sugar to a simmer, stirring frequently to dissolve the sugar. Simmer the mixture, uncovered, until reduced by half, about 10 minutes. Add the garlic and cherry preserves and cook for 1 minute longer. Remove from the heat and let cool. When room temperature, whisk in the red wine vinegar and then the canola oil. Season to taste with salt and pepper. Set aside.

To assemble the salad, in a large bowl, place the mixed baby greens, cherries, and peaches. Whisk the vinaigrette until well blended. Measure 1 cup of the dressing and pour it over the salad. Toss the salad. Season to taste, if needed, with salt and pepper. Transfer the salad to chilled salad bowls, building height in the center. Garnish each salad with a scattering of candied cashews.

Cook's Note: *The Dark Cherry Balsamic Vinaigrette recipe yields about 2½ cups dressing, although you'll only need 1 cup for this salad. Place the extra dressing in a tightly sealed jar and refrigerate for up to 1 month. Use it on other salads, or drizzle it over grilled salmon fillets, shrimp, or lobster.*

Blackened Salmon Caesar

↔ serves 6

Just about everybody loves Caesar salad; it must be the most popular salad in America. This version of the classic has an unusual twist: It's topped with hot, blackened salmon that has been coated with Cajun spices and seared in a hot skillet. In addition, the salad is streaked with a spicy pepper sauce that complements the salmon and garnished with Parmesan cheese that adds a sweet nutty taste. Fair warning, once you make this for your friends and family, they'll be asking for the recipe or, more likely, for you to make it again.

SPICY PEPPER SAUCE

1 cup mayonnaise

Dash of cayenne pepper

Dash of Tabasco sauce

$1/2$ teaspoon paprika

2 teaspoons fresh lemon juice

$1/2$ teaspoon granulated garlic

1 teaspoon chili powder

$1/8$ teaspoon ground cumin

$1/4$ teaspoon kosher salt

1 tablespoon water

CAJUN BLACKENING SPICE

1 tablespoon kosher salt

1 tablespoon sugar

1 teaspoon freshly ground black pepper

2 teaspoons granulated garlic

1 tablespoon granulated onion

1 teaspoon cayenne pepper

2 teaspoons paprika

1 teaspoon dried thyme

1 teaspoon dried oregano

To make the Spicy Pepper Sauce, in a small bowl, combine the mayonnaise, cayenne, Tabasco, paprika, lemon juice, granulated garlic, chili powder, cumin, salt, and water. Whisk until smooth and no lumps remain. Taste and adjust the seasoning. If you are able to find a restaurant-style squeeze bottle, streaking the sauce over the salad makes an attractive presentation. Transfer the sauce to a squeeze bottle or to a covered jar and refrigerate until ready to use. Remove from the refrigerator 20 minutes before serving.

To make the Cajun Blackening Spice, in a small bowl, combine the salt, sugar, pepper, granulated garlic and onion, cayenne, paprika, thyme, and oregano. Mix thoroughly and set aside.

To make the Caesar Dressing, in a bowl, combine the mayonnaise, olive oil, salt, pepper, garlic, anchovy, Parmesan, lemon juice, and Worcestershire sauce. Whisk until smooth. Taste and adjust the seasoning. Cover and refrigerate.

To prepare the salmon, coat both sides of the salmon fillets with some of the Cajun Blackening Spice. Heat a large, heavy skillet, preferably cast iron, over high heat until a bead of water sprinkled in the pan sizzles and evaporates immediately. Add the canola oil, swirl to coat

CAESAR DRESSING

1 cup mayonnaise

2 tablespoons extra-virgin olive oil

$1/2$ teaspoon kosher salt

$1/4$ teaspoon freshly ground black pepper

1 clove garlic, minced

1 olive oil–packed anchovy fillet, patted dry
    and minced

2 tablespoons freshly grated Parmesan cheese,
    preferably Parmigiano-Reggiano

1 tablespoon fresh lemon juice

1 teaspoon Worcestershire sauce

6 salmon fillets (5 ounces each), skin off

2 tablespoons canola oil

2 large heads romaine lettuce, trimmed and
    torn into bite-sized pieces

$1/2$ cup (2 ounces) freshly grated Parmesan cheese,
    preferably Parmigiano-Reggiano, plus more
    for garnish

2 cups homemade or store-bought croutons

3 tablespoons fresh lemon juice

1 lemon, cut into wedges

the bottom of the pan, and then carefully place the salmon fillets in the pan without crowding. (Blacken the salmon fillets in 2 batches, if necessary.) Cook the salmon undisturbed until it blackens on the first side, and then turn the salmon and blacken the other side. Adjust the heat if the salmon is blackening too quickly. Cook the salmon until the fish flakes easily and all translucence is gone, about 3 minutes per side. Remove the skillet from the heat and keep the salmon warm while assembling the salad.

To assemble the salad, pour the Caesar Dressing into a large bowl, top with the romaine, and then the Parmesan, croutons, and lemon juice. Toss the salad until the greens are evenly coated. Season to taste with salt and pepper.

Transfer the salad to chilled salad bowls, building height in the center. Lean a portion of the blackened salmon on each salad. Top each salad with additional Parmesan cheese. Streak each salad, especially the salmon, with some of the Spicy Pepper Sauce. Set a wedge of lemon on the side of each bowl and serve immediately.

Chinese Chicken Salad

→ serves 6

Always looking for new ways to serve chicken salad, the Cafe Nordstrom chefs developed a Chinese variation that, not surprisingly, has become popular. This chicken salad has a sensational layering of textures, colors, and flavors: Crisp greens, a colorful array of julienned vegetables, tender chicken, crunchy nuts, and a shower of crisp wonton strips. When fresh Oregon bay shrimp are in season, they are a wonderful variation, as well.

About 4 cups canola oil for deep-frying

1 package (12 ounces) thin wonton wrappers, about 3¹/₄ inches square

Kosher salt

Freshly ground black pepper

1 large yellow bell pepper, seeded, deribbed, and julienned

1 large red bell pepper, seeded, deribbed, and julienned

1 carrot, peeled and julienned

3 ribs bok choy, greens trimmed and stems cut crosswise into crescents ¹/₄ inch thick

1¹/₄ pounds boneless, skinless chicken breasts, cooked, seasoned with salt and pepper, and julienned

1 can (11 ounces) mandarin orange segments, drained

1 head romaine lettuce, trimmed and torn into bite-sized pieces

10 ounces mixed baby greens

1 cup Ginger-Sesame Dressing (page 22)

¹/₂ bunch cilantro

1 cup (4 ounces) slivered almonds, toasted (see Cook's Note, page 190)

1 tablespoon sesame seeds, toasted (see Cook's Note, page 190)

To fry the wontons, pour the canola oil to a depth of at least 3 inches in a deep saucepan. Place over medium-high heat and heat to 325°F on a deep-frying thermometer. Have ready a rimmed baking sheet lined with a double thickness of paper towels.

While the oil is heating, cut the wontons into strips ¹/₄ inch wide and gently toss to separate the strips. When the oil is ready, add the wonton strips in small batches and fry them until cooked through and light golden brown, 1 to 2 minutes. Using a slotted spoon, transfer the wontons to the prepared baking sheet. Drain and, while still moist with oil, season well with salt and pepper. The wontons can be fried ahead and will hold well for several days at room temperature in an airtight container. (You'll only need about half of the fried wontons for this salad, but they're so good to munch on, it's worth making the whole package.)

To assemble the salad, in a large bowl, place the yellow and red bell peppers, carrot, bok choy, chicken, orange segments, romaine, mixed baby greens, and half of the fried wontons. Drizzle the dressing over the top and toss well to coat all of the ingredients evenly. Season to taste with salt and pepper.

Arrange the salad in chilled salad bowls or plates. Garnish each salad with a few sprigs of cilantro, the remaining fried wontons, and some of the toasted almonds and sesame seeds. Serve immediately.

Pesto Chicken Salad

↬ serves 6

Playing on an Italian theme, this chicken salad is very flavorful and unusual. The chicken is grilled, bringing a smoky charcoal taste that complements the sweetness of the raisins and the nutty flavor brought out by toasting the pine nuts. Combine these three characteristics with the deep flavors of kalamata olives and sun-dried tomatoes, and I promise you rave reviews from friends and family. –ANTHONY MANTUANO

2 pounds boneless, skinless chicken breasts

2 tablespoons extra-virgin olive oil

2 cloves garlic, minced

Kosher salt

Freshly ground black pepper

1 cup homemade or store-bought pesto

$1/4$ cup pine nuts, toasted
    (see Cook's Note, page 190)

$1/4$ cup oil-packed sun-dried tomatoes, cut into
    $1/4$-inch-wide strips

$1/2$ cup golden raisins

$1/4$ cup kalamata olives, pitted and slivered

$1^1/2$ cups firmly packed arugula leaves, stemmed

Prepare a hot fire in a charcoal grill, or preheat a gas grill on high.

Cut the chicken breasts in half and trim away any cartilage and fat. Place the chicken in a bowl and toss with the olive oil, garlic, and a sprinkling of salt and pepper.

Place the chicken directly over the fire. Cover the grill and cook for about 2 minutes. Turn the chicken 90 degrees to create attractive cross-hatching and cook for 2 minutes longer. Flip the chicken breasts over and continue grilling until tender and the juices run clear when the meat is pierced with a knife, about 4 minutes longer. Transfer the chicken to a cutting board, let cool slightly, and then cut into $1/2$-inch cubes.

In a bowl, toss the chicken with the pesto, pine nuts, tomatoes, raisins, and olives. Season to taste with salt and pepper.

Arrange a bed of arugula leaves on each salad plate and spoon some of the chicken salad in the center. Serve immediately.

COOK'S NOTE: *This salad tastes much better if you allow the chicken to char slightly—not burnt, yet a little black.*

SOUPS & STEWS

Acorn Squash Bisque

↔ serves 6 to 8

I call this soup my fall and winter friend. When the leaves start to fall and the air begins to get nippy, it's time to think about acorn squash and one-pot soups and stews. Savory Scones (page 174) are a fantastic accompaniment.
—TONY COLABELLI

4 acorn squash

$^1/_2$ cup (1 stick) plus 2 tablespoons unsalted butter

1 yellow onion, chopped

2 cans (49 ounces each) low-sodium chicken broth

$^3/_4$ cup all-purpose flour

1 teaspoon freshly grated nutmeg

1 teaspoon dried thyme

$1^1/_2$ cups heavy (whipping) cream

$^1/_4$ cup brandy

Kosher salt

Freshly ground black pepper

Preheat the oven to 375°F. Cut each squash in half crosswise. Scoop out and discard the seeds and strings. If necessary, cut a thin slice off the rounded side of each half so that the squash half will sit level. Place the halves on a rimmed baking sheet, hollow-sides up. Fill each squash half with water. Roast until tender when pierced with a knife, 45 minutes to 1 hour. Set aside to cool. When cool enough to handle, drain any water remaining in the squash cavities, scoop out the flesh, and reserve. Discard the skins.

In a 6- to 8-quart saucepan over medium heat, melt 2 tablespoons of the butter. Add the onion and sauté, stirring frequently, until softened, about 3 minutes. Add the chicken broth and bring to a simmer.

Meanwhile, to make the roux that will thicken the soup, melt the remaining butter in a small pan over low heat. Stir in the flour and cook, stirring constantly, until the roux becomes blond, 8 to 10 minutes.

Add the roux to the simmering broth, whisking vigorously until well incorporated. Add the reserved squash flesh and simmer for 25 minutes. Add the nutmeg, thyme, cream, and brandy. Season to taste with salt and pepper. Remove from the heat and purée in a blender or in a food processor fitted with the metal plate until smooth and velvety.

Ladle the soup into a warmed soup tureen or individual bowls and serve immediately.

Winter Lentil Chili

↦ serves 8

For as long as I can remember, weekends around the Peterson house have always been filled with friends and family. When I was growing up, my family had specific meals on specific days. Though it sounds rigid and ritualistic, it actually brought comfort, something you could count on, like football on Sundays and rain all winter in Seattle. Weekend meals, especially Sunday supper, were a big pot of stew or chili. Kept warm on the stove for hours, people would come and go, grabbing a bowl of chili and sitting to watch TV or leaving with a covered container for the long trip home.

This recipe, a Sunday favorite, has been through many changes over the years, and most recently it has gone vegetarian. You won't miss the meat; this chili provides a hearty meal. Serve it with a double batch of Cast-Iron Skillet Corn Bread (page 169). When the word gets out, friends will be stopping by. —MARK PETERSON

2 cups lentils, rinsed and picked over

7 cups water or vegetable broth

1 large yellow onion, finely chopped

2 large red or yellow bell peppers, seeded, deribbed, and finely chopped

2 cans (14.5 ounces each) diced tomatoes in juice

1 can (15 ounces) tomato sauce

¾ cup beer

3 tablespoons chili powder

1 tablespoon ground cumin

2 teaspoons dried oregano

1½ teaspoons cayenne pepper

1½ teaspoons kosher salt

1 cup sour cream

1 cup (4 ounces) shredded Cheddar cheese

In a 6- to 8-quart saucepan, over medium-high heat, combine the lentils and water. Bring to a simmer, reduce the heat to medium-low so the water simmers gently, and cook the lentils until tender, about 45 minutes. Add the onion, bell peppers, tomatoes with juice, tomato sauce, beer, chili powder, cumin, oregano, cayenne, and salt. Stir well, reduce the heat to low, and keep the soup at a bare simmer until the flavors meld, about 30 minutes longer. Taste and adjust the seasoning.

Ladle the chili into warmed bowls and top each serving with a dollop of sour cream and some of the cheese. Serve immediately.

Bistro French Onion Soup

↳ serves 6

French onion soup, although a classic of French cuisine, is actually quite easy to make. If you want to serve this to your friends and family as part of a larger meal, it can be made a day ahead. This makes cooking on the day of a party more relaxed. Serve an easy-to-make main course—the crisp-skinned Bistro Roasted Chicken (page 121) would be perfect— and finish with a delicious dessert, such as the Chocolate Paradise Cake (page 183).

3 tablespoons unsalted butter

3 cloves garlic, minced

4 yellow onions, halved crosswise and thinly sliced

1 leek, white and light green part only, thinly sliced

8 cups canned low-sodium beef broth

$1/8$ teaspoon Tabasco sauce

1 teaspoon Worcestershire sauce

Kosher salt

Freshly ground black pepper

12 baguette slices, each $1/2$ inch thick, toasted

4 cups (1 pound) shredded Gruyère cheese

1 teaspoon snipped fresh chives

In a 6- to 8-quart saucepan over medium heat, melt the butter. Add the garlic and sauté, stirring frequently, until tan, about 1 minute. Add the onions and leek and cook, stirring frequently, until very soft and lightly caramelized, about 30 minutes. Add the broth, bring to a simmer, and simmer for 15 minutes. Add the Tabasco sauce and Worcestershire sauce and season to taste with salt and pepper. Simmer for 10 minutes longer.

While the soup is simmering, position a rack in the upper third of the oven and preheat to 425°F.

Ladle the soup into individual ovenproof crocks. Place 2 baguette slices on top of the soup in each crock. Mound the cheese evenly among the crocks, covering the bread slices completely. Place the crocks on a sturdy, rimmed baking sheet. Bake the soups until the cheese is lightly browned, 10 to 12 minutes.

Carefully remove the baking sheet from the oven and allow the crocks to cool for a few minutes before serving. Garnish each serving with the chives.

Baked Potato Soup

↔ serves 8

The next time you are making baked potatoes, plan ahead and bake a few extra for this hearty and satisfying soup. The topping for each serving includes sour cream, grated Cheddar, crisp bacon, and green onions, a colorful reminder of a "loaded" baked potato. Serve the soup with crusty bread and a simple green salad for a comforting wintertime meal.

3 tablespoons olive oil

3 cloves garlic, minced

1 large yellow onion, chopped

2 carrots, peeled and chopped

2 celery stalks, chopped

1 bay leaf

2 teaspoons dried thyme

1 can (49 ounces) low-sodium chicken broth

5 large baked Idaho potatoes, flesh scooped from the shell and smashed

1 cup heavy (whipping) cream

Kosher salt

Freshly ground black pepper

GARNISH

$^1/_2$ cup sour cream

$^1/_2$ cup (2 ounces) shredded Cheddar cheese

$^1/_4$ cup chopped green onion, including green tops

8 slices bacon, cooked crisp and crumbled

$^2/_3$ cup canned fried shoestring potatoes

In a 6- to 8-quart saucepan over medium heat, warm the olive oil and swirl to coat the bottom of the pan. Add the garlic, onion, carrots, celery, bay leaf, and thyme and sauté, stirring frequently, until the vegetables are softened, about 10 minutes. Add the broth, bring to a simmer, and simmer, uncovered, for 30 minutes. The vegetables should be very tender. Discard the bay leaf. Add the potatoes and simmer for 10 minutes to blend well. Stir in the cream and season to taste with salt and pepper.

Ladle the soup into warmed bowls and garnish each bowl with a dollop of sour cream topped with 1 tablespoon shredded Cheddar, a sprinkling of green onion, and one eighth of the crumbled bacon. Scatter a generous tablespoon of shoestring potatoes around each bowl and serve immediately.

Grandma Goldie's
Chicken Noodle Soup ↔ serves 6 to 8

When I was a little girl, my entire extended family lived in New York City, and we would spend our summers at my grand-parents' cottage on Lake Mohegan in upstate New York. Summers with Grandma Goldie and Grandpa Frank meant swimming in the lake, diving off the floating raft, and eating sweet wild blackberries. I always put up the biggest fight when it was time for dinner. Who wanted to eat dinner when there was still daylight for swimming? When I think back on it, I'm not sure why I wanted to miss a meal; my grandmother was a wonderful cook, and her food, especially her famous chicken soup, always comforted me. It was her secret solution to head colds, including the one I got one summer when I swam at sunset and then walked home dripping wet in the chilly night air. You can save this recipe for when you're sick, but I make it all the time. —CHEF KIMBERLY SCHOR

HOMEMADE CHICKEN STOCK

1 chicken (3^1/$_2$ to 4 pounds)

1 tablespoon vegetable oil or rendered chicken
fat (schmaltz)

1 yellow onion, chopped

3 cups boiling water

2 teaspoons kosher salt

2 bay leaves

CHICKEN NOODLE SOUP

2 tablespoons vegetable oil or rendered chicken
fat (schmaltz)

1 yellow onion, chopped

2 carrots, peeled and cut into ^{1}/$_4$-inch-thick rounds

2 celery stalks, cut crosswise into
^{1}/$_4$-inch-thick slices

^{1}/$_2$ teaspoon dried thyme

2 cups (3 ounces) fine egg noodles

^{1}/$_4$ cup finely chopped fresh parsley

Kosher salt

Freshly ground black pepper

To make the Homemade Chicken Stock, using a cleaver or sharp chef's knife, remove the chicken breast, with the breastbone intact, from the chicken. Cutting through the breastbone, split the breast in half and set aside. As best you can, hack the rest of the chicken into 2-inch pieces.

In a large stockpot over medium-high heat, warm the oil or chicken fat. When it begins to turn hazy, add the breast halves and cook, turning once, until they begin to brown on both sides, about 4 minutes per side. Transfer to a plate and reserve. Add the onion to the pot and cook, stirring frequently, until the onion begins to brown slightly and soften, about 3 minutes. Add the remaining cut-up chicken pieces, and stir continuously until the chicken pieces are no longer pink. Reduce the heat to low, cover the pot, and cook for 20 minutes.

Raise the heat to high and add the boiling water. When the water returns to a boil, add the partially cooked chicken breasts, the salt, and the bay leaves. Reduce the heat so the mixture just simmers and cook, uncovered, for 20 minutes longer. Remove the pot from the heat. Remove the chicken breasts from the pot and set aside to cool. When cool enough to handle, remove and discard the skin and bones, and shred the breast meat into bite-sized pieces. Cover and refrigerate the meat until ready to make the soup.

Strain the stock through a large, fine-mesh sieve, discarding all of the solids. Allow the stock to cool and then cover and refrigerate until the fat solidifies on the surface. When ready to prepare the soup, use a large spoon to skim the chicken fat from the strained stock and reserve for sautéing, if desired (it has great flavor).

To make the Chicken Noodle Soup, in a large stockpot over medium heat, warm the oil or chicken fat. Add the onion, carrots, and celery and cook, stirring frequently, until the vegetables are just beginning to soften, 6 to 8 minutes. Add the thyme, shredded chicken meat, and the reserved stock and simmer until the vegetables are tender, 10 to 15 minutes. Add the noodles and cook until tender, 5 to 7 minutes. Stir in the parsley and season to taste with salt and pepper.

Ladle into warmed soup bowls and serve immediately.

Crispy Tortilla Soup

↔ serves 8

Who can resist a big bowl of soup that has all the flavors of a great taco plate and all the garnishes, too? Chunks of chicken, lots of beans, plus corn and tomatoes swim in a hearty broth scented with cumin, oregano, and cayenne. But the best part is all the toppings: cubes of creamy-ripe avocado, a dollop of sour cream, fresh cilantro leaves, and a mound of crushed tortilla chips. If your friends and family are spice-loving fanatics, serve with a selection of exotic hot-pepper sauces to try with the soup.

2 tablespoons vegetable oil

3 cloves garlic, minced

1 yellow onion, finely chopped

3 cups finely chopped, peeled carrots

$1^{1}/_{2}$ cups finely chopped celery

2 teaspoons ground cumin

Pinch of cayenne pepper

2 teaspoons dried oregano

2 cans (49 ounces each) low-sodium chicken broth

1 can (15 ounces) cooked navy beans,
   drained and rinsed

$1^{1}/_{2}$ pounds boneless, skinless chicken breasts

1 can (14.5 ounces) diced tomatoes in juice

1 cup frozen corn kernels

1 teaspoon Tabasco sauce

2 teaspoons Worcestershire sauce

Kosher salt

Freshly ground black pepper

GARNISH

About $^{1}/_{2}$ cup sour cream

4 cups coarsely crushed tortilla chips

2 ripe avocados

$^{1}/_{2}$ bunch fresh cilantro

2 limes, cut into wedges

In an 8-quart stockpot over medium heat, warm the oil and swirl to coat the bottom of the pan. Add the garlic and sauté until fragrant, less than 1 minute. Add the onion and sauté, stirring occasionally, until the onion begins to brown, 8 to 10 minutes. Add the carrots, celery, cumin, cayenne, and oregano and cook, stirring frequently, until the vegetables have softened, 6 to 8 minutes. Add the broth and the beans, bring to a boil, reduce the heat to low, and simmer for 30 minutes. Add the chicken breasts, turn off the heat, and cover the pot. Let the chicken sit in the hot broth until it is cooked through but still juicy, 15 to 20 minutes, depending on the size of the breasts.

Using tongs or a slotted utensil, transfer the chicken to a cutting board. Add the tomatoes with juice and the corn to the soup and bring it back to a simmer. While it is heating, cut the chicken into small cubes. Add the Tabasco sauce and Worcestershire sauce to the soup, season to taste with salt and pepper, and then add the cubed chicken and heat through.

While the soup is cooking, prepare the garnish. Have ready 8 warmed soup bowls. Place a dollop of sour cream in the center of each bowl and top with $^{1}/_{2}$ cup of the crushed tortilla chips. Cut the avocados into quarters lengthwise, remove the pits, and then remove the peels. Without cutting completely through the avocado at the narrow end, cut each quarter into thin slices and then fan out the slices. Place on top of the tortilla chips.

Carefully ladle the soup into the bowls. Garnish each bowl with 3 or 4 cilantro sprigs. Serve immediately. Pass the lime wedges.

Traditional Meatball Soup

↦ serves 8 to 10

I grew up in Southern California and later worked in East Los Angeles and have eaten a lot of "real" Mexican foods— tacos de carne asada *(grilled beef tacos) and fresh fruit* paletas *(popsicles)—from portable sidewalk carts. Almost twenty years ago a street vendor gave me his prized family recipe for* albondigas *(meatball) soup. Over the years, I have experimented and tweaked the recipe to my liking and have even won cooking contests with this soup. Consider this a colorful meal-in-a-bowl to be shared and savored.* —BOB GELB

MEATBALLS

2 pounds extra-lean ground beef

2 large eggs, lightly beaten

1 cup uncooked Minute Rice

1 tablespoon chopped fresh cilantro

1 teaspoon chopped fresh basil

$1/4$ teaspoon cayenne pepper

$1/4$ teaspoon dried oregano

1 teaspoon kosher salt

To make the meatballs, in a large bowl, mix together the ground beef, eggs, and rice. Add the cilantro, basil, cayenne, oregano, and salt and mix until thoroughly combined. Form into 60 to 65 meatballs, each about 1 inch in diameter. Arrange on a rimmed baking sheet and refrigerate until ready to use.

$1/4$ cup olive oil

4 cloves garlic, minced

2 white onions, chopped

1 red onion, chopped

1 bunch green onions, including green tops,
  chopped

1 small celery stalk, chopped

2 cans (49 ounces each) low-sodium chicken broth

4 cups water

3 tablespoons fresh lemon juice

1 teaspoon paprika

1 teaspoon cayenne pepper

2 tablespoons kosher salt

1 can (15 ounces) garbanzo beans

1 can (15.25 ounces) whole kernel corn

2 cans (15 ounces each) black beans

2 cans (14.5 ounces each) stewed tomatoes

1 cup chopped fresh cilantro

Freshly ground black pepper

GARNISH

About $1/2$ cup sour cream

2 to $2^1/2$ cups coarsely crushed tortilla chips

To make the soup, in an 8-quart saucepan or stockpot over medium-high heat, warm the oil and swirl to coat the bottom of the pan. Add the garlic and sauté, stirring constantly, until golden brown, about 1 minute. Add the white, red, and green onions and the celery and sauté, stirring frequently, until the onions are softened, tender, and sweet, about 10 minutes.

Add the chicken broth and water and bring to a simmer. Reduce the heat to medium and carefully add the meatballs, a few at a time. Return the soup to a gentle simmer and cook for 10 minutes. While the meatballs are cooking, use the side of a spoon to skim off any foam and oil from the surface of the soup.

Gently stir in the lemon juice, paprika, cayenne, and salt. Add the garbanzo beans, corn, black beans, and tomatoes, including the juice from the cans. Raise the heat to high, bring the soup to a boil, and then reduce the heat to a gentle simmer. Cook, uncovered, for about 5 minutes to meld the flavors. Skim the soup of oil and foam three times or so as it cooks. Just before serving, stir in the cilantro and add salt and pepper to taste.

Ladle the soup into warmed bowls. Garnish each serving with a dollop of sour cream and about $1/4$ cup crushed tortilla chips.

Summer Tomato and Basil Soup ↔ serves 8

This is an elegant interpretation of a now-familiar classic. For memorable results buy a high-quality brand of whole, peeled plum tomatoes, such as Italian San Marzano tomatoes. The only downside to this recipe is that you and your friends will be spoiled for life, you'll never be able to enjoy simple canned tomato soup again. If you have the time, try this soup along with freshly baked Focaccia with Olive Oil and Rosemary (page 171) for a special treat. —CHEF TONY COLABELLI

1/3 cup extra-virgin olive oil

5 carrots, peeled and chopped

1 large yellow onion, chopped

1 tablespoon dried basil

2 cans (28 ounces each) whole Italian-style
    tomatoes in purée

2 cans (49 ounces each) low-sodium chicken broth

2 cups heavy (whipping) cream

Kosher salt

Freshly ground black pepper

2 tablespoons lightly packed fresh basil leaves,
    cut into fine ribbons

In a 6- to 8-quart saucepan over medium heat, warm the oil and swirl to coat the bottom of the pan. Add the carrots, onion, and dried basil and sauté, stirring occasionally, until softened, 10 to 12 minutes. Add the tomatoes, including the purée, and the broth and bring just to a boil. Reduce the heat to low and simmer, uncovered, for 20 minutes to blend the flavors.

Remove from the heat. Working in batches, purée the soup in a blender or in a food processor fitted with the metal blade. Return the puréed soup to the saucepan, add the cream, and place over medium heat. Warm until heated through. Season to taste with salt and pepper.

Ladle the soup into a warmed soup tureen or individual bowls, garnish with the basil, and serve immediately.

Stracciatella Soup

↔ serves 10

This simple soup is the Italian equivalent of Chinese egg drop soup. Combining Parmesan cheese with beaten egg whites and then slowly drizzling the mixture into the soup is what makes this recipe unique. For the best results, buy a hunk of Parmigiano–Reggiano, a nutty and flavorful Italian Parmesan, and grate it fresh. Serve the soup with Focaccia with Olive Oil and Rosemary (page 171) warm from the oven and you'll understand true Italian comfort food. —CHEF TONY COLABELLI

3 tablespoons extra-virgin olive oil

3 yellow onions, finely chopped

3 cans (49 ounces each) low-sodium chicken broth

1 chicken ($3^1/4$ pounds), quartered

10 large egg whites

$^1/_2$ cup (2 ounces) freshly grated Parmesan cheese,
   preferably Parmigiano-Reggiano

1 bag (10 ounces) fresh spinach, stems removed

$^1/_2$ cup coarsely chopped fresh basil leaves

Kosher salt

Freshly ground black pepper

In an 8-quart saucepan or stockpot over medium-high heat, warm the oil and swirl to coat the bottom of the pan. Add the onions and sauté, stirring occasionally, until slightly softened and well coated with the oil, about 8 minutes. Add the broth and bring to a simmer. Add the chicken pieces and simmer, uncovered, until the chicken is quite tender, 45 minutes to 1 hour.

Remove the chicken pieces from the broth with a slotted spoon and let cool. Using your fingers or a paring knife, pull the meat from the chicken in fine strands. Discard the skin and bones. Reserve the meat. Thoroughly skim all of the fat from the top of the soup using the side of a spoon.

Bring the soup to a gentle boil. In a 4-cup liquid measuring cup, whisk together the egg whites and Parmesan cheese. Add the spinach and basil to the soup. With the soup gently boiling, add all of the egg white–cheese mixture in a slow, steady stream, whisking the soup continuously. When the mixture is fully is incorporated, add the shredded chicken meat and heat through. Season to taste with salt and pepper.

Ladle the soup into a warmed soup tureen or individual bowls and serve immediately.

Vacation Salmon Chowder

↦ serves 10

There are three reasons this soup is called Vacation Salmon Chowder: one, because there is only one pot to wash and that feels like a vacation from a sink full of dishes; two, because it makes a big batch that leaves plenty for a second meal; and three, because it is a one-bowl meal with some hot, crusty sourdough bread. Take this recipe to the cabin or beach house and have a great vacation.

2 tablespoons extra-virgin olive oil

8 cloves garlic, cut into thin, even slices
   (about $1/4$ cup)

5 carrots, peeled and chopped

6 celery stalks, chopped

2 cans (49 ounces each) low-sodium chicken broth

2 cans (14.5 ounces each) diced tomatoes in juice

1 salmon fillet (about 2 pounds), skinned and
   cut into thirds crosswise

$1/2$ teaspoon Tabasco sauce

1 teaspoon Worcestershire sauce

Kosher salt

Freshly ground black pepper

2 cups lightly packed fresh basil leaves,
   coarsely chopped

In a 6- to 8-quart saucepan over medium-low heat, warm the oil and swirl to coat the bottom of the pan. Add the garlic and sauté, stirring frequently, until the garlic turns light tan, 1 to 2 minutes. Add the carrots and celery and cook, stirring occasionally, until tender, 10 to 12 minutes. Add the broth and the tomatoes with juice, bring to a simmer, and simmer for 25 minutes to blend the flavors.

Carefully lower the salmon into the soup and cook until it flakes easily, about 8 minutes. Using a slotted spoon, transfer the salmon to a plate and let cool. Use the side of a spoon to skim any oil or foam from the surface of the soup. Gently flake the cooled salmon, striving to keep the flakes as large as possible. Return the salmon to the soup and bring back to a simmer over medium heat. Add the Tabasco sauce and the Worcestershire sauce and season to taste with salt and pepper. Stir in the basil.

Ladle the soup into a warmed soup tureen or individual bowls and serve immediately.

San Francisco–Style Cioppino

↔ *serves 8*

This recipe comes from San Francisco's Italian immigrants who created this wonderful stew prepared with tomatoes and a variety of fish and shellfish. Perfect for family gatherings or for entertaining friends, serve the cioppino piping hot on a cool winter evening with a loaf of sourdough bread. —DAVID KIM

1/4 cup extra-virgin olive oil

4 cloves garlic, thinly sliced

2 yellow onions, chopped

1 cup diced celery

1 cup diced green bell pepper

2 tablespoons dried oregano

1 teaspoon dried thyme

1 bay leaf

1 cup dry white wine

3 cans (28 ounces each) whole Italian-style
    tomatoes in juice

2 bottles (8 ounces each) clam juice

1 cooked Dungeness crab, cleaned and cracked
    (2 to 3 pounds)

3/4 pound clams, well scrubbed

3/4 pound mussels, well scrubbed and debearded

8 large shrimp, peeled and deveined

3/4 pound mahi mahi, swordfish, or other
    firm-fleshed fish, cut into 3/4-inch cubes

Kosher salt

Freshly ground black pepper

1/4 cup chopped fresh basil

In a 6- to 8-quart saucepan over medium heat, warm the oil and swirl to coat the bottom of the pan. Add the garlic and sauté, stirring frequently, until the garlic turns light tan, about 1 minute. Raise the heat to medium-high and add the onions, celery, green bell pepper, oregano, thyme, and bay leaf. Cook, stirring occasionally, until the vegetables are slightly softened, 8 to 10 minutes. Add the wine and cook until it evaporates, 3 to 4 minutes. Add the tomatoes with juice, the clam juice, and the crab. Reduce the heat until the liquid just barely simmers, cover, and cook, stirring occasionally, for 25 to 30 minutes to allow the flavors to meld.

Remove the bay leaf and discard it. Add the clams, mussels, shrimp, and fish, discarding any clams or mussels that fail to close to the touch. Simmer until the shellfish and fish are just cooked through, 8 to 10 minutes. Discard any clams or mussels that failed to open. Season to taste with salt and pepper, and stir in the basil.

Ladle the cioppino into warmed bowls and serve immediately.

Bistro Crab Bisque

↣ serves 8

This recipe, which I created, has been on the menu at Nordstrom's Café Bistro since we opened, and there would be protests if we ever took this bisque off the menu. This spicy and satisfying bisque is easy to make at home, perfect for company or for a Sunday–night family supper of bread and soup. —CHEF KIMBERLY SCHOR

2 cooked Dungeness crabs
   (about 2$^1/_2$ pounds each)

5 tablespoons unsalted butter

1 large white onion, chopped

3 carrots, peeled and chopped

4 celery stalks, chopped

1 cup all-purpose flour

4 cloves garlic, smashed with the side of a knife

2 cans (6 ounces) tomato paste

2 cups dry white wine

8 cups water

4 bottles (8 ounces each) clam juice

$^1/_2$ cup brandy

2 cups heavy (whipping) cream

$^1/_8$ teaspoon cayenne pepper

$^1/_2$ teaspoon Tabasco sauce

1 teaspoon kosher salt

1 cup Gazpacho Salsa (page 107)

2 teaspoons snipped fresh chives

Clean and crack the crabs, then remove the meat from the shells. Place the crabmeat in a small bowl, cover, and refrigerate. Use kitchen shears to cut the crab shells into small pieces. Reserve the shells.

In a 6- to 8-quart saucepan over low heat, melt the butter and swirl to coat the bottom of the pan. Add the onion, carrots, and celery and sauté, stirring frequently, until the vegetables are softened, about 12 minutes. Mix in the flour. Add the garlic and crab shells and stir until the crab shells turn bright red, about 8 minutes. Stir in the tomato paste and wine, then stir to combine. Continue cooking for 5 minutes. Add the water and the clam juice and stir to blend the ingredients. Bring the mixture to a simmer and cook, stirring occasionally, for 20 minutes to allow the flavors to meld.

Strain the mixture through a fine-mesh sieve into a clean saucepan, reserving the solids, including the shells. Using a blender, process the solids until finely ground. (This step extracts extra flavor from the shells.) Pour into a fine-mesh sieve lined with cheesecloth placed over a bowl. Pour the brandy and cream over the solids in the sieve. Using the back of a spoon, press down on the solids to extract as much liquid as possible. Add the liquids to the pot holding the strained crab stock.

Add the cayenne, Tabasco sauce, and salt to the pot and bring to a simmer over medium-high heat. Cook until heated through, about 10 minutes. Add the reserved crabmeat. Season to taste with salt and additional cayenne, if desired. Ladle the soup into warmed soup bowls, place 2 tablespoons of Gazpacho Salsa in the center of each serving, and garnish with the chives. Serve immediately.

One-Pan Cajun Jambalaya

↔ serves 4

If you have a spouse or partner who uses every pot and pan in the house when he or she cooks and you are the one who gets to clean up afterward, give your mate this recipe. The result will be a great-tasting dish and just one pan to wash—a happy collaboration! —JOHN PARKER

2 tablespoons unsalted butter

1 yellow onion, chopped

1 yellow bell pepper, chopped

2 cloves garlic, minced

1 pound spicy smoked sausage, preferably andouille, cut into $1/4$-inch-thick slices

1 cup long-grain white rice

2 cups canned low-sodium chicken broth

2 tablespoons Tabasco sauce, or far more for the brave

1 can (14.5 ounces) diced tomatoes in juice

1 tablespoon Cajun seasoning

In a 4- to 6-quart saucepan over medium-high heat, melt the butter and swirl to coat the bottom of the pan. Add the onion, bell pepper, garlic, and sausage and sauté, stirring frequently, until the vegetables are tender, about 7 minutes. Add the rice, broth, Tabasco sauce, tomatoes with juice, and Cajun seasoning. Stir until well mixed and bring to a boil. Reduce the heat to low, cover, and simmer until the rice is tender, 20 to 25 minutes.

Remove from the heat and allow to sit for 5 minutes, then fluff with a fork and serve.

PASTA & RISOTTO

Bucatini with Tomatoes and Pancetta

↔ serves 4 to 6

Bucatini, spaghetti-like but a little stockier and with a hollow core, lends itself to a meaty pasta sauce. I make this dish, which I learned from chef Tony Mantuano, in the fall and winter when I want a substantial, satisfying meal. The recipe calls for pancetta, an Italian-style bacon that is cured with salt and spices, yet not smoked. When preparing this recipe, don't add any salt to the sauce until the dish is finished. Pancetta is quite salty by itself; additional salt may not be necessary.

1 tablespoon kosher salt, plus salt to taste

1 pound bucatini pasta

1/2 pound pancetta, cut into 1/4-inch dice

1 yellow onion, finely chopped

4 cloves garlic, minced

4 cups Garlic Tomato Sauce (page 75)

Freshly ground black pepper

Freshly grated Parmesan cheese, preferably
    Parmigiano-Reggiano, for serving

Fill an 8- to 10-quart stockpot two-thirds full of water and bring to a boil over high heat. Add 1 tablespoon salt to the boiling water, and then add the pasta. Stir and cook the pasta until al dente (cooked through, but still slightly chewy), about 10 minutes.

While the pasta is cooking, make the sauce. In a large sauté pan or skillet over medium heat, sauté the pancetta, stirring occasionally, until most of the fat has been rendered and the pancetta is crisp, 6 to 8 minutes. Drain off all but 3 tablespoons of the fat. Add the onion and garlic and cook, stirring constantly, until the onion is softened and lightly colored, about 4 minutes. Add the Garlic Tomato Sauce and simmer for 3 to 4 minutes. Set aside and keep warm.

Drain the pasta in a colander, but do not rinse, and then return it to the pasta cooking pot. Pour 3 cups of the sauce over the top and toss gently. Season to taste with salt and pepper.

Divide the pasta among warmed bowls, spoon some of the remaining sauce over each serving, and garnish with a little Parmesan cheese. Serve immediately.

Farfalle with Snow Peas and Asparagus → serves 6

Here is a light and refreshing pasta dish perfect for spring entertaining. The simple sauce, which is similar to an Alfredo, is prepared in a single pan with a minimum of effort.

3 tablespoons extra-virgin olive oil

2 cloves garlic, minced

3/4 pound pencil-thin asparagus, tough ends removed and cut into 1 1/2-inch lengths

1/2 pound snow peas, stems and strings removed

1 tablespoon kosher salt, plus salt to taste

Freshly ground black pepper

3 cups heavy (whipping) cream

1 cup (4 ounces) freshly grated Parmesan cheese, preferably Parmigiano-Reggiano, plus more for garnish

1 pound dried farfalle pasta

Fill an 8- to 10-quart stockpot two-thirds full of water and bring to a boil over high heat.

Meanwhile, in a large skillet over medium-low heat, warm the olive oil and garlic. Sauté the garlic, stirring constantly, until it turns a light tan, about 1 minute. Add the asparagus and snow peas, raise the heat to medium, and sauté the vegetables, stirring constantly, until they turn bright green and are crisp-tender, 4 to 6 minutes. Season to taste with salt and pepper. Add the cream and simmer until the sauce is reduced by half, about 3 minutes, then stir in the 1 cup Parmesan cheese. The sauce should coat the back of a spoon. Remove from the heat, set aside, and keep warm.

Add 1 tablespoon salt to the boiling water and then add the pasta. Stir and cook the pasta until al dente (cooked through, but still slightly chewy), about 10 minutes. Drain the pasta in a colander, but do not rinse, and return it to the pasta cooking pot. Pour the sauce over the top and toss gently. Taste and adjust the seasoning.

Divide the pasta among warmed bowls, sprinkle a little cheese over the top, and serve immediately.

Orecchiette with Chicken, Caramelized Onions, and Blue Cheese ↦ serves 4 to 6

One of the pleasures of working in the restaurant business is mixing work with play. Travel for work means dining out often, tasting other cuisines, and discovering new dishes and flavor combinations. Once home, we like to play in the kitchen, re-creating favorite dishes. This pasta dish is one of those discoveries turned into a favorite. —VICKI AND BILL WILSON

2 tablespoons unsalted butter

5 tablespoons extra-virgin olive oil

4 yellow onions, quartered and thinly sliced

1 1/2 pounds boneless, skinless chicken breasts

1 tablespoon kosher salt, plus salt to taste

Freshly ground black pepper

1 pound orecchiette pasta

1 tablespoon chopped fresh rosemary

1 1/2 cups (6 ounces) crumbled blue cheese

In a large skillet over medium-high heat, melt the butter and 4 tablespoons of the olive oil. Add the onions, reduce the heat to medium, and cook, stirring frequently, until the onions are soft, richly browned, and caramelized, 20 to 25 minutes. Remove from the heat and keep warm.

While the onions are cooking, prepare a hot fire in a charcoal grill or preheat a gas grill on high. Pound the chicken lightly between 2 pieces of plastic wrap to a uniform 1/4-inch thickness. Rub the chicken with the remaining 1 tablespoon olive oil and season well with salt and pepper.

Place the chicken about 4 inches from the broiler or directly over the fire. If using a grill, cover it and cook on one side for about 4 minutes. Flip the chicken breasts over and continue cooking, covered if using a grill, until tender and the juices run clear when the meat is pierced with a knife, about 4 minutes longer. Set aside while the pasta cooks.

Fill an 8- to 10-quart stockpot two-thirds full of water and bring to a boil over high heat. Add 1 tablespoon of salt to the boiling water, and then add the pasta. Stir and cook the pasta until al dente (cooked through, but still slightly chewy), about 10 minutes.

While the pasta is cooking, cut the chicken into 1/2-inch-wide strips and place in a large, warmed serving bowl. Sprinkle the chicken with the rosemary and toss to combine. Drain the pasta in a colander, but do not rinse, then add to the bowl along with the blue cheese. Toss to combine, cover, and set aside briefly until the cheese partially melts. Add the caramelized onions to the bowl, toss to combine, and season to taste with salt and pepper. Serve immediately.

Gemelli with Smoked Turkey and Arugula ↔ serves 4 to 6

This recipe pairs peppery, aromatic arugula with smoked turkey for this memorable pasta. Buy the turkey at a deli so that you can specify extra-thick slices. This way, the turkey can easily be cut into matchsticks for adding to the sauce. A crisp green salad and garlic toast hot from the oven are good accompaniments. —CHEF TONY COLABELLI

1¼ cups (about 4 ounces) dry-packed
    sun-dried tomatoes

Boiling water

1 tablespoon kosher salt, plus salt to taste

1 pound gemelli pasta

¼ cup extra-virgin olive oil

3 cloves garlic, finely minced

1 yellow bell pepper, seeded, deribbed,
    and chopped

¾ pound thickly sliced smoked turkey breast,
    cut into 2-inch-by-¼-inch matchsticks

3 cups heavy (whipping) cream

2 cups firmly packed arugula leaves
    and tender stems

Freshly ground black pepper

Freshly grated Parmesan cheese, preferably
    Parmigiano-Reggiano, for serving

In a bowl, soak the sun-dried tomatoes in boiling water to cover until softened, about 10 minutes. Drain the tomatoes and coarsely chop.

Fill an 8- to 10-quart stockpot two-thirds full of water and bring to a boil over high heat. Add 1 tablespoon salt to the boiling water, and then add the pasta. Stir and cook the pasta until al dente (cooked through, but still slightly chewy), about 10 minutes.

While the pasta is cooking, heat the olive oil in a large skillet over low heat. Add the garlic and sauté, stirring constantly, until it turns light tan, about 1 minute. Add the bell pepper, raise the heat to medium, and cook, stirring often, until softened, 3 to 4 minutes. Add the turkey and the sun-dried tomatoes and sauté, stirring frequently, for 2 to 3 minutes. Add the cream and simmer until the cream is reduced by half and coats the back of a spoon, about 2 minutes. Add the arugula and cook, stirring constantly, until the arugula has wilted, about 1 minute.

Drain the pasta in a colander, but do not rinse, then return it to the pasta cooking pot. Pour the sauce over the top and toss gently. Season to taste with salt and pepper.

Divide the pasta among warmed bowls, sprinkle a little cheese over the top, and serve immediately.

Penne with Smoked Salmon, Peas, and Cream ↔ serves 4 to 6

Typically, I serve this pasta as part of a Sunday brunch or as a light dinner main course. The European (especially Scottish) smoked salmon will work in this dish, but alder-smoked salmon from the Pacific Northwest is the best choice. Alder-smoking provides more flavor and the texture is a little drier, making it perfect for this recipe. —CHEF DAVID SHAW

1 tablespoon unsalted butter

$1/2$ cup thinly sliced leek, white and light green

    parts only

$1/2$ cup diced yellow bell pepper

2 cups heavy (whipping) cream

$1/4$ pound smoked salmon, thinly sliced

1 cup frozen petite peas, thawed

1 tablespoon kosher salt, plus salt to taste

1 pound penne pasta

Freshly ground black pepper

Freshly grated Parmesan cheese,

    preferably Parmigiano-Reggiano, for serving

Fill an 8- to 10-quart stockpot two-thirds full of water and bring to a boil over high heat.

Meanwhile, in a large skillet over medium heat, melt the butter and swirl to coat the bottom of the pan. Add the leek and bell pepper and sauté, stirring frequently, until tender, about 4 minutes. Add the cream and simmer until the sauce is reduced by one third, about 15 minutes. Reduce the heat to low, add the salmon and peas, and cook until heated through, 2 to 3 minutes. Set aside and keep warm.

Add 1 tablespoon salt to the boiling water and then add the pasta. Stir and cook the pasta until al dente (cooked through, but still slightly chewy), about 10 minutes. Drain the pasta in a colander, but do not rinse, and then return it to the pasta cooking pot. Pour the sauce over the top and toss gently. Season to taste with salt and pepper.

Divide the pasta among warmed bowls, sprinkle a little cheese over the top, and serve immediately.

Pasta Carbonara

↪ serves 4 to 6

On those wintry evenings when we arrive home late, and we're tired and hungry, an easy pasta dish with a simple green salad and a glass of our favorite Pinot Noir is what we want. Pasta carbonara has always been a comfort-food favorite for my wife and me. This is my recipe for that well-known dish, with a few embellishments. —PAUL CARR

1 tablespoon kosher salt, plus salt to taste

1 pound farfalle pasta

1/2 pound high-quality, thick-cut bacon, coarsely chopped

1 yellow onion, chopped

1/2 pound button mushrooms, stems trimmed and sliced 1/4-inch thick

2 cups heavy (whipping) cream

1/4 cup (1 ounce) crumbled blue cheese

3/4 cup (3 ounces) freshly grated Parmesan cheese, preferably Parmigiano-Reggiano

1 cup frozen peas, thawed

2 large egg yolks

Freshly ground black pepper

Fill an 8- to 10-quart stockpot two-thirds full of water and bring to a boil over high heat. Add 1 tablespoon salt to the boiling water, and then add the pasta. Stir and cook the pasta until al dente (cooked through, but still slightly chewy), about 10 minutes.

While the pasta is cooking, make the sauce. In a large sauté pan or skillet over medium heat, sauté the bacon, stirring occasionally, until most of the fat has been rendered and the bacon is crisp, 6 to 8 minutes. Drain off all but 3 tablespoons of the bacon fat. Add the onion and mushrooms and cook, stirring constantly, until the onion is softened and lightly colored, about 4 minutes. Add the cream, bring to a simmer, and cook until the sauce begins to thicken, about 4 minutes. Add the blue cheese and half of the Parmesan and stir to combine. Add the peas, stir, and then remove from the heat. Place the egg yolks in the center of the sauce and stir in rapidly, not allowing the egg yolks to cook before combining with the sauce.

Drain the pasta in a colander, but do not rinse, and return it to the pasta cooking pot. Pour the sauce over the top and toss gently. Season to taste with salt and pepper.

Divide the pasta among warmed bowls, garnish evenly with the remaining Parmesan, and serve immediately.

Angel Hair Pasta with
Garlic Tomato Sauce and Pesto ↦ serves 4 to 6

Every cook needs a great tomato sauce in his or her cooking repertoire. Here is my favorite—simple, rustic, and full of rich tomato flavor. This sauce is packed with thinly sliced and browned garlic and a hearty addition of fresh basil. The sauce complements the thin, delicate angel hair pasta wonderfully, and a dollop of pesto adds yet more color and punch.

GARLIC TOMATO SAUCE

2 tablespoons extra-virgin olive oil

8 cloves garlic, cut into thin, even slices
(about $1/4$ cup)

2 cans (28 ounces each) whole Italian-style
tomatoes in purée

$1/4$ cup coarsely chopped fresh basil

Kosher salt

Freshly ground black pepper

1 tablespoon kosher salt

1 pound angel hair pasta

Freshly ground black pepper

4 to 6 tablespoons homemade or
store-bought pesto

4 to 6 fresh basil leaves

Freshly grated Parmesan cheese, preferably
Parmigiano-Reggiano, for serving

To make the Garlic Tomato Sauce, in a 4-quart saucepan over medium-low heat, warm the oil and swirl to coat the bottom of the pan. Add the garlic and sauté, stirring constantly, until it turns light tan, about 1 minute. Add the tomatoes, including the purée, and simmer, stirring occasionally, until the sauce thickens and the flavors meld, 10 to 15 minutes. Using the back of a spoon or a potato masher, break up the whole tomatoes into chunky pieces. Add the basil and season to taste with salt and pepper.

While the sauce is cooking, fill an 8- to 10-quart stockpot two-thirds full of water and bring to a boil over high heat. Add 1 tablespoon salt to the boiling water, and then add the pasta. Stir and cook the pasta until al dente (cooked through, but still slightly chewy), 6 to 8 minutes. Drain the pasta in a colander, but do not rinse, and then return it to the pasta cooking pot. Pour 2 cups of the sauce over the top and toss gently. Season to taste with salt and pepper.

Divide the pasta among warmed bowls. On each serving, spoon a "stripe" of additional sauce across the top, place a dollop of pesto in the center and garnish with a basil leaf. Serve immediately. Pass the Parmesan cheese at the table.

Pasta Puttanesca

↔ serves 4 to 6

The Wilberton family meals rely heavily on pantry staples. Keeping pasta, olive oil, capers, anchovies, olives, garlic, and tomatoes in ready supply makes interesting, spur-of-the-moment meals possible. This recipe is a perfect example. In the middle of winter on a snowy night, I'd much rather be cooking in my warm kitchen than running to the store for ingredients. –JULIE WILBERTON

1/4 cup extra-virgin olive oil

5 cloves garlic, minced

2 to 3 olive oil-packed anchovy fillets, patted dry
   and minced (optional)

2 tablespoons capers, drained and rinsed

1/2 cup pitted kalamata olives, halved
   (save the brine)

1/2 cup pitted green olives, halved

1 can (28 ounces) whole Italian-style tomatoes
   in juice, drained and coarsely chopped

1 tablespoon kosher salt, plus to taste

1 pound fusilli pasta

5 ripe plum tomatoes, cored and chopped
   (about 2 cups)

1 tablespoon chopped fresh flat-leaf parsley

1 tablespoon chopped fresh basil

Freshly ground black pepper

Freshly grated Parmesan cheese, preferably
   Parmigiano-Reggiano, for serving

Place a large sauté pan or skillet over medium-low heat. Add the oil, garlic, and anchovies and sauté until heated through, being careful not to brown the garlic, 1 to 2 minutes. Add the capers and the kalamata and green olives. Heat through and then add the canned tomatoes. Bring to a gentle boil, adjust the heat, and allow to simmer while the pasta cooks.

Fill an 8- to 10-quart stockpot two-thirds full of water and bring to a boil over high heat. Add 1 tablespoon salt to the boiling water, and then add the pasta. Stir and cook the pasta until al dente (cooked through, but still slightly chewy), about 10 minutes. Drain the pasta in a colander, but do not rinse.

While the pasta is draining, add the plum tomatoes to the sauce and heat through without letting the fresh tomatoes break down. (The sauce should be a little loose. If the sauce has thickened too much, add a little of the kalamata olive brine or a bit of water to thin it.) Add the pasta, parsley, and basil to the sauce and toss gently to mix. Season to taste with salt and pepper.

Divide the pasta among warmed bowls, sprinkle a little cheese over the top, and serve immediately.

Cheese Ravioli with Fresh Spinach and Mushrooms ⇸ serves 6 to 8

Here is an easy pasta, which is good for a crowd, whether planned or spur-of-the-moment. Use your favorite brand of fresh or frozen ravioli. Mushrooms can be found all year long but are best in the spring and fall. Substitute or vary the mushrooms according to what you like. The Garlic Tomato Sauce goes together quickly, or if you are lucky, you have some already prepared. —CHEF DAVID SHAW

1 tablespoon kosher salt, plus salt to taste

2 pounds fresh or frozen cheese ravioli

$1/4$ cup extra-virgin olive oil

3 cloves garlic, minced

$1/4$ pound oyster mushrooms, stems trimmed

$1/4$ pound shiitake mushrooms, stems removed and thinly sliced

$1/4$ pound button mushrooms, stems trimmed and quartered

$1/4$ pound cremini mushrooms, stems trimmed and quartered

1 bag (10 ounces) fresh baby spinach, stems removed

4 cups Garlic Tomato Sauce (page 75)

Freshly ground black pepper

$1/2$ cup (2 ounces) crumbled feta cheese

Fill an 8- to 10-quart stockpot two-thirds full of water and bring to a boil over high heat. Add 1 tablespoon salt to the boiling water, and then add the ravioli. Stir and cook the ravioli according to package directions until al dente (cooked through, but still slightly chewy).

While the water is heating, start the sauce. In a large sauté pan or skillet over low heat, warm the olive oil. Add the garlic and sauté, stirring constantly, until it turns light tan, about 1 minute. Raise the heat to medium-high, add the mushrooms, and sauté, stirring occasionally, until well browned, 2 to 3 minutes. Add the spinach and the Garlic Tomato Sauce and simmer until the spinach is wilted and the sauce is heated through, 3 to 4 minutes. Season to taste with salt and pepper.

Drain the ravioli in a colander, but do not rinse, and return them to the pasta cooking pot. Pour half of the sauce over the top and toss gently.

Divide the ravioli among warmed bowls and spoon the remaining sauce over the top. Garnish each portion with some of the feta cheese and serve immediately.

Mom's Baked Ziti

↦ serves 6

Having raised a large family of eight children, I learned to make all of the meals from scratch to keep within my budget. Likewise, I found it wise to be economical with time so that I wasn't chained to the stove trying to prepare big meals. Now when my children and grandchildren come to visit I try to do much of the work before everyone arrives. This recipe is great because almost everything can be done in advance, with the dish simply being baked in the oven when company arrives. –KATHERINE LANTZ

MOM'S TOMATO SAUCE

2 tablespoons olive oil

1 yellow onion, chopped

1 clove garlic, minced

2 cans (15 ounces each) tomato sauce

1 can (6 ounces) tomato paste

2 teaspoons light brown sugar

Kosher salt

Freshly ground black pepper

1³⁄₄ tablespoons kosher salt

1 pound ziti pasta

1 pound lean ground beef

1 container (15 ounces) ricotta cheese

1 large egg, lightly beaten

¹⁄₄ teaspoon freshly ground black pepper

¹⁄₄ cup chopped fresh flat-leaf parsley

2 cups (¹⁄₂ pound) shredded mozzarella cheese

To make Mom's Tomato Sauce, in a 4-quart saucepan over medium heat, warm the oil and swirl to coat the bottom of the pan. Add the onion and garlic and sauté, stirring occasionally, until the onion is softened, about 5 minutes. Stir in the tomato sauce, tomato paste, and brown sugar, reduce the heat to low, and simmer, uncovered, for 15 to 20 minutes to meld the flavors. Season to taste with salt and pepper. Set aside.

Fill an 8- to 10-quart stockpot two-thirds full of water and bring to a boil over high heat. Add 1 tablespoon salt to the boiling water, and then add the pasta. Stir and cook the pasta until al dente (cooked through, but still slightly chewy), about 10 minutes. Drain and rinse the pasta in a colander. Set aside.

To assemble the dish, preheat the oven to 350°F. In a large Dutch oven over medium heat, cook the ground beef, breaking up the meat with the back of a spoon, until browned, about 5 minutes. Remove from the heat and drain off the fat. Stir in the ricotta, egg, the remaining ³⁄₄ teaspoon salt, pepper, and parsley. Add half of the tomato sauce and mix to combine. Gently fold in the cooked pasta. Transfer to a 9-by-13-inch glass baking dish, and level the mixture lightly with the back of a spoon. Pour the remaining tomato sauce over the top and sprinkle with the mozzarella.

Bake, uncovered, until hot and bubbly, 20 to 25 minutes. Serve immediately.

Butternut Squash Risotto
with Fresh Sage ↦ serves 4 as a main course

The inspiration for this recipe came from pumpkin-filled tortellini with brown butter and sage, a classic northern Italian pasta dish. Here, I'm stirring cubes of butternut squash into the risotto and then garnishing the dish with crisp sage leaves fried in butter and crushed amaretti cookies. This makes a perfect fall supper.

4 cups finely diced, peeled butternut squash

1 can (49 ounces) low-sodium chicken broth

4 tablespoons ($^1/_2$ stick) unsalted butter

1 star anise

16 whole fresh sage leaves, stems removed

$^3/_4$ cup finely diced white onion

2 cups Arborio rice

$^1/_2$ cup dry white wine

$^1/_2$ cup (2 ounces) freshly grated Parmesan cheese, preferably Parmigiano-Reggiano, plus more for garnish (optional)

1 cup coarsely crumbled amaretti cookies

Kosher salt

Freshly ground pepper

Place the diced squash in a steamer above an inch or so of boiling water. Cover and steam the squash just until tender when pierced with a fork, about 8 minutes.

Bring the broth just to a simmer in a 3-quart saucepan. In a heavy 4-quart saucepan over medium heat, melt 3 tablespoons of the butter. Add the star anise and stir for 1 minute to flavor the butter. Add the sage leaves and fry, stirring to coat both sides of the leaves, until lightly crisped, 1 to 2 minutes. Using a slotted spoon, transfer the fried sage leaves to a plate lined with paper towels and set aside. Remove and discard the star anise. Add the onion and sauté until translucent but not brown, about 3 minutes. Add the rice and stir until the grains are well coated with the butter, about 2 minutes. Add the wine, let it come to a boil, and then cook, stirring constantly, until the wine mostly evaporates.

Add $^1/_2$ cup of the broth to the rice and cook, stirring frequently, until the rice has almost completely absorbed the liquid. Keep the heat at a slow simmer. Repeat, adding $^1/_2$ cup of the broth at a time, always waiting until it is almost fully absorbed before adding more. Reserve $^1/_4$ cup broth for adding at the end. After about 18 minutes, the rice will be plump, creamy, and cooked through but still slightly chewy. Add the remaining $^1/_4$ cup broth, the squash, the remaining 1 tablespoon butter, the $^1/_2$ cup Parmesan cheese, and half of the amaretti cookie crumbs. Season to taste with salt and pepper.

Spoon the risotto into warmed shallow bowls. Garnish each serving with some of the fried sage leaves, the remaining cookie crumbs, and the additional Parmesan cheese, if desired. Serve immediately.

Roasted Cauliflower Risotto

↔ *serves 4 as a main course*

While traveling in northern Italy, I ate this simple dish at a four-hundred-year-old rice mill outside of Verona. The chef prepared a seven-course meal that day, all risottos. The Veronese in attendance had a contest to see who could guess which rice variety was used in each risotto. I wrote down the ingredients for this recipe before the chef and I sat drinking grappa long into the night! No guessing needed on the rice: Buy Arborio rice imported from Italy. —RICHARD LADD

1 white onion, thinly sliced, plus $1/2$ cup
    finely diced white onion

4 cloves garlic, halved

1 small head (about $1^1/2$ pounds) cauliflower,
    trimmed of green parts

3 tablespoons extra-virgin olive oil

Kosher salt

Freshly ground black pepper

1 can (49 ounces) low-sodium chicken broth

4 tablespoons ($1/2$ stick) unsalted butter

2 cups Arborio rice

$1/2$ cup dry white wine

$1/2$ cup (2 ounces) freshly grated Parmesan
    cheese, preferably Parmigiano-Reggiano,
    plus more for garnish (optional)

Preheat the oven to 325°F. Scatter the sliced onion and the garlic in the bottom of a baking dish and top with the cauliflower. Drizzle with oil and season with salt and pepper. Cover with aluminum foil and roast until the cauliflower is tender when pierced with a knife, about 1 hour. Discard the onion and garlic. Transfer the cauliflower to a cutting board. Cool the cauliflower slightly, and then gently smash the cauliflower into medium-sized pieces with the back of a wooden spoon. Reserve.

About 15 minutes before the cauliflower is finished cooking, start the risotto. Bring the broth to a low simmer in a 3-quart saucepan. In a heavy 4-quart saucepan over medium heat, melt 3 tablespoons of the butter. Add the diced white onion and sauté until translucent but not brown, about 3 minutes. Add the rice and stir until the grains are well coated with the butter, about 2 minutes. Add the wine, let it come to a boil, and then cook, stirring constantly, until the wine mostly evaporates.

Add $1/2$ cup of the broth to the rice and cook, stirring frequently, until the rice has almost completely absorbed the liquid. Adjust the heat so the risotto is kept at a slow simmer. Repeat, adding $1/2$ cup of the broth at a time, always waiting until it is almost fully absorbed before adding more. Reserve $1/4$ cup broth for adding at the end. After about 18 minutes, the rice will be plump, creamy, and cooked through but still slightly chewy. Stir the cauliflower into the rice mixture, and then add the remaining $1/4$ cup broth, the $1/2$ cup Parmesan cheese, and the remaining 1 tablespoon butter. Season to taste with salt and pepper. Spoon the risotto into warmed shallow bowls and serve immediately. Garnish with additional Parmesan cheese, if desired.

Risotto alla Milanese

↔ serves 4 as a main course

When I serve risotto at a dinner party, guests always ask about the rice and the stirring process required for perfect risotto. The kernels of the Arborio rice used for making risotto are shorter and fatter than those of other types of rice. The shape and high starch content of the rice, along with the constant stirring and slow addition of liquid are what give risotto its classic creamy texture. In this recipe, the richness of the beef broth and the scent of saffron complement the creamy rice, and the garnish of freshly grated Parmesan rounds out the dish with a nutty sweetness.

1 can (49 ounces) low-sodium beef broth

$1/2$ teaspoon saffron threads

3 tablespoons unsalted butter

1 white onion, finely diced

2 cups Arborio rice

$1/2$ cup dry white wine

$1/2$ cup (2 ounces) freshly grated Parmesan
    cheese, preferably Parmigiano-Reggiano,
    plus more for garnish (optional)

Kosher salt

Freshly ground black pepper

Bring the broth and the saffron threads to a very gentle simmer in a 3-quart saucepan. In a heavy 4-quart saucepan over medium heat, melt 2 tablespoons of the butter. Add the onion and sauté until translucent but not brown, about 3 minutes. Add the rice and stir until the grains are well coated with the butter, about 2 minutes. Add the wine, let it come to a boil, and then cook, stirring constantly, until the wine mostly evaporates.

Add $1/2$ cup of the broth to the rice and cook, stirring frequently, until the rice has almost completely absorbed the liquid. Adjust the heat so the risotto is kept at a slow simmer. Repeat, adding $1/2$ cup of the broth at a time, always waiting until it is almost fully absorbed before adding more. Reserve $1/4$ cup broth for adding at the end. After about 18 minutes, the rice will be plump, creamy, and cooked through but still slightly chewy. Add the remaining $1/4$ cup broth, the $1/2$ cup Parmesan cheese, and the remaining 1 tablespoon butter. Season to taste with salt and pepper.

Spoon the risotto into warmed shallow bowls and serve immediately. Garnish with additional Parmesan cheese, if desired.

Risotto with Shrimp, Asparagus, and Shiitake Mushrooms → serves 4 as a main course

This risotto dish celebrates the arrival of spring produce. It includes the earthy flavors of tender asparagus and buttery shiitake mushrooms, both of which complement the sweet shrimp. Make this risotto in the early spring when tender, pencil-thin asparagus are in the market.

2 tablespoons olive oil

2 cloves garlic, minced

1/2 pound shiitake mushrooms, stems removed and diced

3/4 pound pencil-thin asparagus, tough ends removed and cut into 1/4-inch lengths

Kosher salt

Freshly ground black pepper

1 can (49 ounces) low-sodium chicken broth

4 tablespoons (1/2 stick) unsalted butter

1/2 cup finely diced white onion

2 cups Arborio rice

1/2 cup dry white wine

1 pound shrimp peeled, deveined, and coarsely chopped

1/2 cup (2 ounces) freshly grated Parmesan cheese, preferably Parmigiano-Reggiano, plus more for garnish (optional)

In a large skillet over medium-high heat, warm the oil and swirl to coat the bottom of the pan. Add the garlic and mushrooms and sauté until the mushrooms begin to brown, 2 to 3 minutes. Add the asparagus and cook, stirring constantly, until the asparagus is tender, about 2 minutes longer. Season to taste with salt and pepper, then remove from the heat and set aside.

Bring the broth just to a simmer in a 3-quart saucepan. In a heavy 4-quart saucepan over medium heat, melt 3 tablespoons of the butter. Add the onion and sauté until translucent but not brown, about 3 minutes. Add the rice and stir until the grains are well coated with the butter, about 2 minutes. Add the wine, let it come to a boil, and then cook, stirring constantly, until the wine mostly evaporates.

Add 1/2 cup of the broth to the rice and cook, stirring frequently, until the rice has almost completely absorbed the liquid. Adjust the heat so the risotto is kept at a slow simmer. Repeat, adding 1/2 cup broth at a time and always waiting until it is almost fully absorbed before adding more. Reserve 1/4 cup broth for adding at the end. After about 18 minutes, the rice will be plump, creamy, and cooked through but still slightly chewy. Stir in the shrimp along with the mushroom mixture and cook until the shrimp are cooked through, about 2 minutes. Add the remaining 1/4 cup broth, the remaining 1 tablespoon butter, and the 1/2 cup Parmesan cheese. Season to taste with salt and pepper.

Spoon the risotto into warmed shallow bowls. Garnish each serving with additional Parmesan cheese, if desired. Serve immediately.

FROM THE GRILL

Homemade Barbecue Sauce

↦ makes about 8 cups

I'm going to do a little boasting here. I've spent a lot of time around grills, and I have yet to find a sauce, prepared or homemade, that beats this one. It is so good that I suggest you make the big batch this recipe yields. It keeps for at least three months in the refrigerator, but rather than hoard it, pack it into mason jars and give it as gifts to family and friends. Feel free to kick up the heat level, if you wish, by adding more black pepper, red pepper flakes, or cayenne—or add more of all of them!

2 tablespoons kosher salt

1 tablespoon granulated garlic

1 teaspoon onion powder

1^1/$_2$ teaspoons freshly ground black pepper

1 tablespoon sugar

1 teaspoon red pepper flakes

^{1}/$_2$ teaspoon ground cumin

^{1}/$_4$ teaspoon dried oregano

^{1}/$_4$ teaspoon ground ginger

^{1}/$_8$ teaspoon ground mace

^{1}/$_8$ teaspoon ground allspice

^{1}/$_8$ teaspoon cayenne pepper

Pinch of ground cloves

3 cups water

3 cups light corn syrup

^{3}/$_4$ cup cider vinegar

4 cans (6 ounces each) tomato paste

6 tablespoons dark molasses

2 tablespoons Worcestershire sauce

1 tablespoon liquid smoke

^{1}/$_4$ cup Dijon mustard

To make a dry spice seasoning mixture, thoroughly combine the salt, granulated garlic, onion powder, black pepper, sugar, red pepper flakes, cumin, oregano, ginger, mace, allspice, cayenne, and cloves. Set aside.

In a 4- to 6-quart saucepan over medium-low heat, combine the water and corn syrup and bring to the barest simmer, stirring occasionally. Whisking constantly, add the dry spice seasoning mixture to the pan along with the vinegar. Continuing to whisk, add the tomato paste and cook for 4 minutes. Add the molasses, Worcestershire sauce, liquid smoke, and mustard and whisk to combine. Simmer, stirring occasionally, until the sauce begins to thicken and coats the back of a spoon, about 25 minutes.

Remove from the heat and let cool to room temperature. Transfer to jars with tight-fitting lids and refrigerate for up to 3 months.

Corey's Chipotle Barbecue Jam

↦ makes about 3 quarts

While working as a sous-chef at Jubilanté restaurant outside of Seattle, I came to be known as the Chipotle King because of my love for smoky, spicy chipotle chiles. The regular customers called the restaurant Corey's Chipotle Corner because they could count on me to feature chipotle chiles in just about everything I made. It's also where I developed my best barbecue sauce, Chipotle Barbecue Jam. It is thick, sweet, and spicy, but if you want it even spicier, add a few extra chipotles. —COREY NIPERT

1/4 cup extra-virgin olive oil

6 cloves garlic, minced

3 Walla Walla or Vidalia onions (about 1 1/2 pounds),
    finely grated

4 cups tomato paste

1 can (14.5 ounces) low-sodium beef broth

3 cups dark molasses

3 cups cider vinegar

3 cups firmly packed dark brown sugar

1 1/2 cups Worcestershire sauce

1/3 cup chili powder

3 canned chipotle chiles in adobo sauce, puréed
    (see Cook's Note)

In a 6-quart saucepan over medium heat, warm the oil and swirl to coat the bottom of the pan. Add the garlic and onions and sauté, stirring frequently, until the onions are translucent and tender, about 7 minutes. Add the tomato paste and cook, stirring frequently, until the onion-tomato mixture has a rusty color and sweet aroma, about 5 minutes. Reduce the heat to low and add the beef broth, molasses, vinegar, brown sugar, Worcestershire sauce, chili powder, and chipotle chiles. Cook, stirring frequently, until the sauce thickens, about 20 minutes.

Remove from the heat and let cool to room temperature. Transfer to jars with tight-fitting lids and refrigerate for up to for 3 months.

COOK'S NOTE: *Look for canned chipotle (smoke-dried jalapeños) drenched in adobo sauce (made from ground chiles, herbs, and vinegar) in Latin markets or in the Mexican-food section in supermarkets.*

Hoisin Barbecue Glaze

↝ makes 2½ cups

As an alternative to the American–style barbecue sauces included in this book, I thought it would be fun to offer an Asian-style finishing sauce. This is the type of sauce that gets slathered on ribs, chicken, shrimp, steaks, and even vegetables right before they are ready to come off the grill. There are lots of brands of hoisin on the market; some are of better quality than others. One of my favorites is Koon Chun because of its jamlike consistency and sweet quality. Hoisin sauce will keep indefinitely in the refrigerator.

2 tablespoons vegetable oil

3 cloves garlic, minced

1 tablespoon peeled and minced fresh ginger

1 tablespoon Chinese chile sauce with garlic
  (see Cook's Note)

½ cup rice wine vinegar

¼ cup soy sauce

2 cups hoisin sauce

½ cup chopped fresh cilantro

In a 2-quart saucepan over medium-low heat, warm the oil and swirl to coat the bottom of the pan. Add the garlic, ginger, and chile sauce and cook, stirring constantly, until the mixture becomes fragrant and heated through, about 1 minute. Add the vinegar and reduce until nearly evaporated, about 5 minutes. Reduce the heat to low, add the soy sauce and hoisin, and cook, stirring constantly, until well blended, about 5 minutes. If the sauce seems too thick, adjust it with a little water to the desired consistency.

Remove from the heat and let cool to room temperature. Add the cilantro to the cooled sauce and stir until well blended. Use immediately, or store in a jar with a tight-fitting lid in the refrigerator for up to 2 weeks.

Cook's Note: *Chinese chile sauce with garlic is a bright-tasting, thick sauce found in cans or jars in Asian grocery stores or well-stocked supermarkets.*

Cooper's Barbecue Sauce

↔ makes about 8 cups

When my son, Cooper, was young, I wanted to teach him how to cook. What better way to start, I thought, than with the typical male bonding ritual of barbecue. Cooper's Barbecue Sauce is terrific with Perfect Barbecued Chicken (page 101) and great on ribs, pork tenderloin, and even salmon. Nowadays, we get carried away when we cook together and always make lots of food. In the case of this sauce, that's fine, since our friends are always asking for jars of sauce to take home.

—CHEF DAVID AND COOPER SHAW

1 tablespoon ground allspice

1 tablespoon cayenne pepper

1/2 cup paprika

1 tablespoon dry mustard

2 cups Irish whiskey

1 1/2 cups red wine vinegar

1 cup molasses

2 cups firmly packed dark brown sugar

1 1/2 cups ketchup

1/2 cup fresh lemon juice

1/4 teaspoon liquid smoke

In a heavy 4-quart saucepan over low heat, combine the allspice, cayenne, paprika, and mustard. Toast the spices, stirring constantly, until they are fragrant, about 4 minutes. Raise the heat to medium and add the whiskey, vinegar, molasses, brown sugar, and ketchup. Cook for 4 minutes or until lightly boiling. Reduce the heat to low and cook, stirring occasionally, until the sauce coats the back of a spoon, about 20 minutes.

Remove from the heat and let cool to room temperature. Add the lemon juice and liquid smoke and stir until blended. Transfer to jars with tight-fitting lids and refrigerate for up to 3 months.

Italian Grilled Vegetables

↦ serves 6 to 8

Grilled vegetables, whether served as a starter to a summer dinner on the deck or arranged on a buffet for an outdoor party, make a splashy, colorful presentation. This dish is perfect for entertaining since the vegetables taste great either warm or at room temperature. Once you have tasted the Sun-Dried Tomato Vinaigrette, my hunch is that it will become a pantry staple. Drizzled over the grilled vegetables, this dressing completes the dish with a sweet yet tangy finish.

1 pound jumbo asparagus

2 zucchini, cut lengthwise into $^{1}/_{2}$-inch-thick slices

1 eggplant, cut crosswise into $^{1}/_{2}$-inch-thick slices

2 summer squash, cut lengthwise into
$^{1}/_{2}$-inch-thick slices

4 plum tomatoes, cored and halved

1 large yellow bell pepper, seeded, deribbed,
and cut into $^{1}/_{2}$-inch-thick rings

1 large red bell pepper, seeded, deribbed,
and cut into $^{1}/_{2}$-inch-thick rings

3 portobello mushrooms, stems and black gills
removed, then halved

$^{1}/_{3}$ cup extra-virgin olive oil

Kosher salt

Freshly ground black pepper

1 cup Sun-Dried Tomato Vinaigrette (page 32)

Prepare a medium-hot fire in a charcoal grill, or preheat a gas grill on medium-high.

Snap off the woody bottom end of each asparagus spear, then trim any ragged edges, or trim the spears to a uniform length. Using a vegetable peeler, lightly peel the bottom half of each spear, removing only the thin, fibrous outer layer.

Lay the asparagus and all the remaining vegetables in a single layer on 2 rimmed baking sheets. Brush on both sides with the olive oil and season with salt and pepper.

Place the vegetables in a single layer directly over the medium hot fire. Grill the vegetables on one side just until grill marks appear, about 3 minutes. Turn and grill until tender but still firm, 2 to 3 minutes longer.

Remove the vegetables from the grill and arrange them attractively on a large serving platter. Stir the Sun-Dried Tomato Vinaigrette to combine, then streak it all over the grilled vegetables. Serve hot or at room temperature.

Grilled Chicken Chardonnay

↦ serves 8

Marinades penetrate deeply to improve the flavor and succulence of foods, especially chicken breasts. This simple combination of olive oil, Chardonnay, lemon juice, rosemary, and oregano imparts crisp, clean flavors to the meat that are enhanced by the smoky flavors from grilling. Accompany the chicken with Italian Grilled Vegetables (page 93).

8 boneless, skinless chicken breast halves

1 cup extra-virgin olive oil

3/4 cup Chardonnay

1/4 cup fresh lemon juice

3 cloves garlic, finely chopped

2 tablespoons coarsely chopped fresh rosemary

1 tablespoon dried oregano

2 teaspoons kosher salt

1 teaspoon freshly ground black pepper

Vegetable oil for brushing

Place the chicken in a 1-gallon lock-top plastic bag or in a shallow baking dish. In a bowl, combine the olive oil, wine, lemon juice, garlic, rosemary, oregano, salt, and pepper, and whisk until thoroughly blended. Pour the marinade over the chicken, coating all sides well. Squeeze all the air out of the bag and seal it, or cover the dish. Refrigerate and marinate the chicken a minimum of 4 hours or for up to 24 hours. Turn the bag or the chicken breasts once to distribute the flavors evenly. Remove from the refrigerator 30 minutes prior to grilling.

Prepare a medium fire in a charcoal grill, or preheat a gas grill on medium.

Remove the chicken from the marinade and drain the chicken of excess marinade. Brush the grill grate with vegetable oil. Place the chicken directly over the fire. Cover the grill and cook on one side for about 2 minutes. Turn the chicken about 90 degrees to create attractive cross-hatching and cook for 2 minutes longer. Flip the chicken breasts over and continue grilling, covered, until tender and the juices run clear when the meat is pierced with a knife, about 4 minutes longer. Serve immediately.

Summer Grilled Citrus Chicken

↬ serves 8

That old saying "Necessity is the mother of invention" was certainly true when I was taking care of a sick friend and needed to cook dinner from whatever was in the house. The surprising part is that this "throw-it-together" dish has become a favorite and frequently requested recipe of my family and friends. Serve the chicken with a big green salad and some fresh corn hot off the grill. —LYSSA CRIPE

8 boneless, skinless chicken breast halves

1 1/4 cups fresh orange juice

1/2 cup fresh lemon juice

1/3 cup fresh lime juice

2 shallots, minced

1 clove garlic, minced

1/3 cup rice wine vinegar

1/4 cup extra-virgin olive oil

2 teaspoons kosher salt

1/2 teaspoon freshly ground black pepper

Vegetable oil for brushing

Place the chicken in a 1-gallon lock-top plastic bag or in a shallow baking dish. In a bowl, combine the orange, lemon, and lime juices, shallots, garlic, vinegar, oil, salt, and pepper, and whisk until thoroughly blended. Pour the marinade over the chicken, coating all sides well. Squeeze all the air out of the bag and seal it, or cover the dish. Refrigerate and marinate for up to 12 hours. Turn the bag or the chicken breasts once to distribute the flavors evenly. Remove from the refrigerator 30 minutes prior to grilling.

Prepare a medium fire in a charcoal grill, or preheat a gas grill on medium.

Remove the chicken from the marinade and drain the chicken of excess marinade. Brush the grill grate with vegetable oil. Place the chicken directly over the fire. Cover the grill and cook on one side for about 2 minutes. Turn the chicken about 90 degrees to create attractive cross-hatching and cook for 2 minutes longer. Flip the chicken breasts over and continue grilling, covered, until tender and the juices run clear when the meat is pierced with a knife, about 4 minutes longer. Serve immediately.

Authentic Jerk Chicken

↔ serves 4 to 6

Any recipe for jerk paste, the fiery soul-satisfying seasoning rub from Jamaica, certainly includes all the traditional ingredients—ginger, garlic, onion, lime juice, allspice, thyme, and a mega dose of chiles—but the cook almost always personalizes the concoction. My version kicks up the number of green onions and uses a heavy hand with the spices, but keeps the chiles as a background note. Feel free to experiment, especially with the chiles. Jerk paste is especially good on chicken and pork, although a light coating on halibut or shrimp is terrific, too. This recipe is typically used as a wet rub but, if blended with additional liquid, can work as a marinade. —DAVID KIM

1 bunch green onions, including green tops, cut into 1-inch lengths

6 quarter-sized slices fresh ginger, peeled

4 cloves garlic

3 jalapeño chiles, including seeds and ribs, quartered (see Cook's Note)

3 bay leaves, crumbled

2 tablespoons fresh thyme leaves

$1/4$ cup fresh lime juice

$1/4$ cup peanut or vegetable oil

1 tablespoon freshly ground black pepper

1 tablespoon ground coriander

1 tablespoon kosher salt

2 teaspoons ground allspice

1 teaspoon freshly grated nutmeg

1 teaspoon ground cinnamon

1 chicken ($3^1/2$ pound), quartered

Vegetable oil for brushing

In a food processor fitted with the metal blade, combine the green onions, ginger, garlic, chiles, bay leaves, and thyme; process to a coarse paste. Add the lime juice, oil, pepper, coriander, salt, allspice, nutmeg, and cinnamon; process until combined. Use immediately, or transfer to a jar with a tight-fitting lid and refrigerate for up to 2 days.

Place the chicken on a rimmed baking sheet and rub all over with the jerk paste, coating thoroughly. Set aside to marinate while the grill preheats.

Prepare a medium fire in a charcoal grill, or preheat a gas grill on medium.

Brush the grill grate with vegetable oil. Place the chicken, skin-side down, directly over the fire. Cover the grill and cook on one side for about 12 minutes. Flip the chicken over and continue grilling, covered, until the juices run clear when a thigh is pierced with a knife or until an instant-read thermometer inserted into the thickest part of the breast and thigh registers 165°F, about 12 minutes longer. Serve immediately.

Cook's Note: *For those who like their jerk paste kickin' hot, substitute 3 Scotch bonnet or habanero chiles, including the seeds, for the jalapeños.*

Thai Chicken Satay Skewers

↔ serves 4 to 6

I first fell in love with satay while stationed in Thailand in the U.S. Navy in 1981. It was an eye-opening experience for a twenty-year-old kid from a small ranching community in Northern California. Satay is a staple in the street stalls of every market and soi *(back street) in Thailand. Exposure to the many wonderful cuisines of the world during my travels in the military directly contributed to my desire to become a chef. The healthful, lean ingredients and clean flavors of Southeast Asian cooking continue to be a major influence in my cooking, both professionally and at home.* —PATRICK ROBERTSON

MARINADE

$1/2$ cup Thai fish sauce *(nam pla)*

$1/4$ cup soy sauce

3 tablespoons Asian sesame oil

$1/4$ cup firmly packed light brown sugar

1 tablespoon peeled and minced fresh ginger

1 tablespoon minced fresh garlic

Grated zest of 3 limes

1 lemongrass stalk, tender inner bulb only,
     finely chopped

2 tablespoons minced jalapeño chile,
     including seeds

1 tablespoon curry powder

$1/4$ cup finely chopped fresh cilantro stems

$2^1/2$ pounds boneless, skinless chicken breasts,
     cut across the grain into $3/4$-inch-wide strips

12 ten-inch bamboo skewers

To make the marinade, in a large bowl, combine the fish sauce, soy sauce, sesame oil, brown sugar, ginger, garlic, lime zest, lemongrass, jalapeño, curry, and cilantro. Whisk to combine. Place the chicken in the bowl and toss to coat evenly. Cover and refrigerate for 4 to 8 hours, stirring occasionally to keep the chicken pieces coated. Meanwhile, soak twelve 10-inch bamboo skewers in water for 2 hours.

To make the Peanut Sauce, in a small saucepan over medium heat, warm the peanut oil. Add the shallots, ginger, garlic, lemongrass, and jalapeño and sauté until just beginning to color, about 4 minutes. Add the lime juice, fish sauce, peanut butter, and coconut milk. Cook, stirring constantly, until the sauce is well combined, about 3 minutes. Remove from the heat and set aside. Thin with a little water if the sauce becomes too thick.

To make the Cucumber Salad, in a small saucepan over medium-high heat, combine the vinegar, fish sauce, water, and sugar. Bring to a boil, stirring frequently, until the sugar dissolves, about 3 minutes. Place the cucumber and jalapeño in a heatproof bowl and pour the boiling

continued

PEANUT SAUCE

$1/4$ cup peanut oil

2 small shallots, finely chopped

1 tablespoon peeled and minced fresh ginger

2 cloves garlic, minced

$1/2$ lemongrass stalk, tender inner bulb only,
    finely chopped

2 teaspoons minced jalapeño chile, including seeds

Juice of 3 limes (about $1/4$ cup)

$1/4$ cup Thai fish sauce *(nam pla)*

2 cups peanut butter, creamy or chunky

1 cup unsweetened coconut milk

CUCUMBER SALAD

$1/2$ cup white vinegar

$1/2$ cup Thai fish sauce *(nam pla)*

$1/2$ cup water

$1/2$ cup sugar

1 large English cucumber, ends trimmed, quartered
    lengthwise, and then cut crosswise into
    $1/8$-inch-thick slices

1 jalapeño chile, seeded, deribbed, and thinly sliced

Leaves from $1/2$ bunch fresh cilantro, chopped

Vegetable oil for brushing

mixture over the top. Stir until the cucumbers are well coated. Let cool slightly, then add the cilantro. Cover and refrigerate until ready to serve.

Drain the skewers. Remove the chicken from the marinade and divide evenly among the skewers. Weave the chicken strips onto the skewers. Using the flat side of a meat mallet, gently flatten the meat. Leave at room temperature while you prepare the grill.

Prepare a medium-hot fire in a charcoal grill, or preheat a gas grill on medium-high.

Brush the grill grate with vegetable oil. Place the skewers directly over the fire. Cover the grill and cook on one side for 2 to 3 minutes, checking occasionally to make sure the chicken isn't burning. Turn and cover again. Cook until the chicken is tender and cooked through, about 3 minutes longer.

Arrange on a platter and serve with the Peanut Sauce and the Cucumber Salad.

Perfect Barbecued Chicken

↦ *serves 4 to 6*

I credit the success of this recipe for barbecued chicken to brining. Soaking the bird in a brine overnight ensures that it will not only be plump and moist, but also permeated with flavor. You can choose your favorite sauce to slather on the bird just before it comes off the grill, but my son, Cooper, and I are partial to Cooper's Barbecue Sauce. Serve the chicken with Summer Corn Salad with Champagne Vinaigrette and Plum Tomatoes (page 24). —CHEF DAVID SHAW

1 chicken (3^1/$_2$ pound), cut into 8 pieces

^{1}/$_2$ cup sugar

^{1}/$_3$ cup kosher salt

1 tablespoon allspice berries

1 tablespoon black peppercorns

3 dried red chiles

1 bay leaf

1 piece cinnamon stick (2 inches)

6 cups water

Vegetable oil for brushing

1^1/$_2$ to 2 cups Cooper's Barbecue Sauce (page 92)

To brine the chicken, place the chicken in a large plastic container with a tight-fitting lid or in a 1^1/$_2$-gallon lock-top plastic bag.

In a 2-quart saucepan, combine the sugar, salt, allspice, peppercorns, chiles, bay leaf, cinnamon stick, and water. Bring to a boil over high heat, stirring occasionally to dissolve the sugar and salt. Reduce the heat to low, cover, and simmer for 20 minutes. Remove from the heat and let cool completely. Pour the brine over the chicken, covering it completely. Cover the container or press all the air out of the bag, seal it, and place in it a bowl. Refrigerate and brine the chicken for 12 hours.

Prepare a medium-low fire in a charcoal grill, or preheat a gas grill on medium-low.

Remove the chicken from the brine, rinse under running cold water, and then pat dry with paper towels. Brush the grill grate with vegetable oil. Place the chicken, skin-side down, directly over the fire. Cover the grill and cook on one side for about 12 minutes, checking occasionally to make sure the chicken isn't burning. Flip the chicken pieces over and continue grilling, covered, until tender and the juices run clear when a thigh is pierced with a knife, about 12 minutes longer. Brush generously with the barbecue sauce just before removing from the grill. Serve immediately or keep warm until serving.

Asian Grilled Chicken Wings with Lemongrass → serves 4

This sweet and spicy marinade is packed with the wonderful ingredients used in Southeast Asian cooking—garlic, shallot, ginger, lemongrass, turmeric, peanuts, and fish sauce. Easy to prepare, boldly flavored, and quick to grill, this dish makes summer entertaining a breeze. —DAVID KIM

3 cloves garlic

1 shallot, halved

2 quarter-sized slices fresh ginger, peeled

2 lemongrass stalks, tender inner bulb only,
    coarsely chopped

1 teaspoon paprika

$1/2$ teaspoon ground turmeric

$1/2$ cup water

2 tablespoons Thai fish sauce *(nam pla)*

3 tablespoons sugar

2 teaspoons kosher salt

2 tablespoons chopped roasted peanuts

2 pounds chicken wing drumettes

Vegetable oil for brushing

In a food processor fitted with the metal blade, combine the garlic, shallot, ginger, lemongrass, paprika, turmeric, and water; process to a smooth paste.

In a large bowl, combine the resulting paste with the fish sauce, sugar, salt, and peanuts. Add the chicken drumettes, and then toss to combine. Cover and marinate in the refrigerator overnight. Stir the chicken once to distribute the flavors evenly. Remove from the refrigerator 30 minutes prior to grilling.

Prepare a medium fire in a charcoal grill, or preheat a gas grill on medium.

Remove the chicken from the marinade and drain the chicken of excess marinade. Brush the grill grate with vegetable oil. Place the chicken directly over the fire. Cover the grill and cook on one side for about 5 to 6 minutes. Flip the drumettes over and continue grilling, covered, until tender and the juices run clear when a drumette is pierced with a knife, about 5 to 6 minutes longer. Serve immediately or keep warm until serving.

Jack's Dry Rub Barbecued Salmon

↔ serves 8 to 10

My friend Jack Rosling shared this recipe with me. Jack gets his family together as often as he can in the summer for big salmon barbecues. He experiments with different rubs and marinades for the salmon; this rub is one of his favorites. Shop for the freshest wild salmon you can find and serve the salmon with baked or fried potatoes and a big tossed salad.
—CHEF DAVID SHAW

1 cup firmly packed light brown sugar

1 tablespoon paprika

1 tablespoon chili powder

1 tablespoon garlic powder

1 teaspoon kosher salt

$1/2$ teaspoon freshly ground black pepper

$1/2$ teaspoon cayenne pepper

$1/2$ teaspoon ground coriander

$1/2$ teaspoon ground cumin

2 salmon fillets (about 5 pounds total), skin on

Vegetable oil for brushing

To make the dry rub, in a small bowl, stir together the brown sugar, paprika, chili powder, garlic powder, salt, black pepper, cayenne, coriander, and cumin.

Prepare a medium fire in a charcoal grill, or preheat a gas grill on medium.

Place the salmon fillets, skin-side down, on heavy-duty aluminum foil cut a little larger than the fillets. Rub the flesh side of each salmon fillet with half of the dry rub. Using the foil as a cradle, place the salmon on the foil directly over the fire. Cover the grill and cook on one side for 6 to 8 minutes. Meanwhile, prepare a second sheet of heavy-duty aluminum foil, cut a little larger than the fillets, this time brushing the foil generously with vegetable oil so that the fish will not stick. When the fillets are ready on the first side, cover them with the second sheet of foil, oiled-side down, and carefully flip the fillets over. Remove the foil that was on the skin side of the fillets. Continue grilling, covered, until opaque throughout and the fish flakes easily when tested with a fork, about 4 minutes.

Using two wide spatulas, lift each salmon fillet from the foil, flipping it skin-side down onto a warmed serving platter. Serve immediately.

Grilled Whole Striped Bass

↔ serves 4

Many cooks think preparing whole fish is complicated and challenging. Nothing could be further from the truth. Whole fish, especially when grilled, tend to be moister and more tender than fillets. Although this recipe calls for striped bass, other whole fish, such as red snapper, can be substituted with equal success. In addition to using the freshest fish, the other secrets to making this simple—yet incredibly delicious—dish are using a high-quality extra-virgin olive oil and fresh herbs.

2 whole striped bass (1^1/$_2$ pounds each),
   cleaned with heads on

4 cloves garlic, minced

2 tablespoons fresh rosemary leaves

1^1/$_4$ cups extra-virgin olive oil

3 teaspoons kosher salt

1 teaspoon freshly ground black pepper

Vegetable oil for brushing

2 tablespoons chopped flat-leaf parsley

^{1}/$_4$ cup fresh lemon juice

^{1}/$_4$ teaspoon freshly ground white pepper

Ask your fishmonger to trim off all the fins and the thinnest portion of the tail so that it won't burn on the grill. Before marinating the fish, rinse it well and cut several deep incisions, on an angle, through the flesh and to the bone on both sides of the fish. This allows the marinade to penetrate and shortens the cooking time. Lay the fish flat in a shallow baking dish.

To make the marinade, combine the garlic, rosemary, ^{3}/$_4$ cup of the olive oil, 2 teaspoons of the salt, and the black pepper. Whisk to blend thoroughly. Pour the marinade over the fish, coating all sides well. Cover the dish. Refrigerate and marinate for 4 to 6 hours. Turn the fish once to distribute the flavors evenly. Remove from the refrigerator 30 minutes prior to grilling.

Prepare a medium fire in a charcoal grill, or preheat a gas grill on medium. Remove the fish from the marinade and drain the fish of excess marinade. Brush the grill grate with vegetable oil. Place the fish directly over the fire. Cover the grill and cook on one side for 10 to 12 minutes. Carefully turn the fish over and continue grilling, covered, until the translucence is gone and the flesh separates easily from the bone, 10 to 12 minutes longer.

Once the fish has been turned, drizzle a large, warmed platter with the remaining ^{1}/$_2$ cup olive oil. Sprinkle the parsley over the top, and then add the lemon juice, the remaining 1 teaspoon salt, and the white pepper. Gently stir together with a fork. Remove the fish from the grill and place it into the pool of olive oil. Turn the fish to coat both sides. Bone the fish, discarding the head and backbone, and serve immediately.

Grilled Salmon with
Gazpacho Salsa ↦ serves 6

Salmon is an easy fish to grill because its flesh remains firm and intact throughout the cooking. If possible, buy wild salmon rather than farm-raised, which pales in comparison. The wild salmon are all from the West Coast, while much of the Atlantic salmon is farm-raised. The peak season for wild salmon is from late spring through summer, ideal for the grilling season. Special varieties include king, Alaskan king, Copper River king, sockeye, and coho.

The cool, refreshing flavors of the Gazpacho Salsa are a perfect complement to the rich smoky flavors of the grilled salmon. This recipe works equally well with pan-seared salmon that is finished by baking in the oven.

GAZPACHO SALSA

8 plum tomatoes, cored, seeded, diced, and drained

1 small cucumber, peeled, seeded, and diced

3 green onions, including green tops,
    finely chopped

$1/2$ cup diced red onion

1 yellow bell pepper, seeded, deribbed, and diced

3 tablespoons red wine vinegar

$1/2$ cup extra-virgin olive oil

$1/4$ cup fresh lemon juice

$1/2$ cup ketchup

1 teaspoon Worcestershire sauce

$1/2$ teaspoon Tabasco sauce

Kosher salt

Freshly ground black pepper

$2 1/2$ pounds salmon fillet, skinned and cut into
    6 equal portions, each about 4 inches square

2 tablespoons olive oil

Kosher salt

Freshly ground black pepper

Vegetable oil for brushing

To make the Gazpacho Salsa, in a large bowl, combine the tomatoes, cucumber, green onions, red onion, bell pepper, vinegar, olive oil, lemon juice, ketchup, Worcestershire sauce, and Tabasco sauce. Season to taste with salt and pepper. Mix thoroughly, cover, and refrigerate until ready to serve.

Prepare a medium fire in a charcoal grill, or preheat a gas grill on medium.

Rub the salmon pieces with a light amount of olive oil and season well with salt and pepper. Brush the grill grate generously with vegetable oil. Place the salmon directly over the fire. Cover the grill and cook on one side until a spatula inserted under the fish easily lifts the fillet, about 4 minutes. Turn the salmon about 90 degrees to create attractive cross-hatching and cook for 1 minute longer. Carefully flip the salmon over and continue grilling, covered, until opaque throughout and the fish flakes easily when tested with a fork, about 4 minutes.

Using a wide spatula, transfer the salmon to warmed dinner plates. Spoon about $1/2$ cup of the Gazpacho Salsa over each portion of grilled salmon and serve immediately.

Grilled Butterflied Leg of Lamb

↦ serves 10

I was introduced to this recipe by my Greek neighbors. Ask your butcher to bone and butterfly the lamb and to remove the excess fat, which will otherwise drip onto the fire and causes flare-ups. Serve the lamb with an assortment of grilled vegetables, especially strips of red bell peppers and slices of sweet onions and hot pita bread. —LINDSAY CARPENTER

1 boned and butterflied leg of lamb (4 to 5 pounds)

2 cloves garlic, crushed

$1/4$ teaspoon peeled and minced fresh ginger

1 tablespoon extra-virgin olive oil

1 cup dry red wine

$3/4$ cup canned low-sodium beef broth

3 tablespoons orange marmalade

3 tablespoons red wine vinegar

$1^1/2$ tablespoons dried marjoram

$1^1/2$ tablespoons dried rosemary

$1^1/2$ tablespoons dried thyme

1 bay leaf, crumbled

1 teaspoon kosher salt

Vegetable oil for brushing

Lay the butterflied lamb leg flat on a cutting board, skin-side up. Trim away any skin and fat. Place the lamb in a shallow baking dish large enough to hold it flat. Set aside.

In a small saucepan over low heat, combine the garlic, ginger, and olive oil. Sauté stirring constantly, until the garlic is light tan, about 1 minute. Add the wine, broth, marmalade, vinegar, marjoram, rosemary, thyme, bay leaf, and salt and stir well. Simmer, uncovered, until slightly reduced, about 20 minutes. Remove from the heat and let cool completely. When cool, pour the mixture over the leg of lamb. Cover the dish. Refrigerate and marinate for 8 to 10 hours or overnight, turning at least once.

About 1 hour before grilling, remove the lamb from the refrigerator and then remove it from the marinade. Pour the marinade into a small saucepan and bring to a boil over high heat. Return the heat to medium and simmer for 3 to 4 minutes. Remove from the heat and set aside.

Prepare a medium-low fire in a charcoal grill, or preheat a gas grill on medium-low. Brush the grill grate with vegetable oil. Place the lamb, fatty-side down, directly over the fire. Cover the grill and cook on one side for 15 minutes, brushing occasionally with the reserved marinade. Turn the lamb and grill, again brushing occasionally with the marinade, until an instant-read thermometer inserted into the thickest part registers 125° to 130°F for rare or 145° to 150°F for medium, 15 to 20 minutes longer. Transfer the lamb to a carving board, tent it loosely with aluminum foil, and allow it to rest for 15 minutes. Thinly slice the lamb on a slight diagonal across the grain. Serve immediately.

Steak au Poivre

↔ *serves* 4

All you need to make this classic and easy-to-prepare peppered steak dish is a heavy, well-seasoned cast-iron skillet. This style of cooking is called flat-top grilling, a searing technique that is regularly used in restaurants. For the best flavor, crack whole peppercorns fresh. Use either a spice grinder, or place the peppercorns in a heavy lock-top plastic bag and crack them using the bottom of a sturdy skillet.

COGNAC CREAM SAUCE

1 tablespoon olive oil

1 shallot, minced

1 clove garlic, minced

$^1/_2$ teaspoon black peppercorns

$^1/_4$ cup cognac

1 can (14.5 ounces) low-sodium beef broth

2 cups (1 pint) heavy (whipping) cream

4 New York strip steaks
    (each about 10 ounces and 1 inch thick)

Kosher salt

2 tablespoons cracked black pepper

2 tablespoons extra-virgin olive oil

To make the Cognac Cream Sauce, in a small saucepan over medium heat, warm the oil and swirl to coat the bottom of the pan. Add the shallot and garlic and sauté, stirring frequently, until the shallot is softened and beginning to brown, about 3 minutes. Add the peppercorns and cognac and cook until the Cognac is nearly evaporated. Add the broth and bring to a boil. Reduce the heat to medium-low and simmer until the broth is reduced by half. Remove from the heat and pour through a fine-mesh sieve. Return to the saucepan and simmer until reduced to about 6 tablespoons. Reduce the heat to low and stir in the cream. Use a rubber spatula to incorporate any of the reduced sauce sticking to the sides of the pan. Cook over low heat until the sauce is reduced by half and coats the back of a spoon, about 10 minutes. Remove from the heat and keep warm.

Heat a large, heavy skillet, preferably cast-iron, over high temperature. Season the steaks well with salt. Press the cracked peppercorns into both sides of each steak. When the skillet is hot (a drop or two of water will dance on the surface), add the olive oil and then the steaks. Cook, uncovered, until the steaks are seared and brown on the first side, 5 to 6 minutes. Turn the steaks over and cook until an instant-read thermometer registers 120°F for rare or 130° to 135°F for medium-rare, 4 to 5 minutes longer.

Place the steaks on warmed dinner plates. Pool one fourth of the sauce around each steak, and serve immediately.

Tuscan-Style Sliced Steak

↔ serves 4

In Tuscany, steaks are charcoal grilled, sliced, and then dressed with the finest Tuscan olive oil, cracked black pepper, fresh rosemary, and lemon juice. The flavors are divine; the steaks are delicious. As the steaks come off the grill, enlist some help from friends and family to carve and dress them.

4 New York Strip steaks (each about 10 ounces
    and 1 inch thick), well trimmed

2 cloves garlic, minced

Kosher salt

Freshly ground black pepper

2 teaspoons black peppercorns, cracked

Vegetable oil for brushing and drizzling

$1/2$ cup high-quality Tuscan extra-virgin olive oil

1 tablespoon fresh rosemary leaves,
    leaves separated

$1^{1}/2$ lemons, quartered

Prepare a medium fire in a charcoal grill, or preheat a gas grill on medium.

While the grill is preheating, rub the steaks with the garlic and season generously with salt and ground pepper. Set aside. Place the peppercorns in a lock-top plastic bag, squeeze out the air, and seal the bag. Using the bottom of a heavy skillet, crush the peppercorns by pressing down hard on them and rocking the heel of the pan back and forth until they are cracked but not pulverized. (Take the time to do this step, as store-bought cracked pepper tastes harsh, bitter, and flavorless.)

Brush the grill grate with vegetable oil. Place the steaks directly over the fire. Grill the steaks on one side for 5 minutes for rare to 7 minutes for medium-rare. Flip the steaks over and cook until an instant-read thermometer registers 120°F for rare or 130° to 135°F for medium-rare, 4 minutes or longer, or until done to your liking. Transfer the steaks to a carving board and let rest for 5 minutes.

Using a sharp knife, cut the steaks across the grain at a 45-degree angle, slicing each steak into 7 slices. Transfer each steak to a warmed dinner plate, fanning out the slices. Drizzle each steak with some of the olive oil, sprinkle with some of the cracked pepper, scatter some of the rosemary leaves over the top, and then add a squeeze of lemon juice and a dash of salt. Serve immediately.

Maple-Chipotle Barbecued Pork Chops → *serves 4*

For this recipe, I use Homemade Barbecue Sauce to glaze the pork chops, but bring the flavor of the sauce up a bit by adding chipotle chiles and maple syrup. You may need to special order double–bone pork chops from your butcher. Ask the butcher to remove the second bone, but make sure he leaves the other bone intact and frenches it (removes all the meat, fat, and connective tissue from the bone). Serve the pork chops accompanied with Maple Roast Acorn Squash (page 156) or Gruyère and Custard Baked Potatoes (page 164).

4 double-bone center-cut loin pork chops, about
    2^1/$_2$ inches thick (see recipe introduction)

2 cloves garlic, finely minced

Kosher salt

Freshly ground black pepper

1 teaspoon ground cumin

1 cup Homemade Barbecue Sauce (page 89)

^{1}/$_4$ cup pure maple syrup

1 teaspoon finely minced canned chipotle chiles
    in adobo sauce (see Cook's Note, page 90)

Vegetable oil for brushing

Rub the pork chops with the garlic and season generously with salt and pepper. Wrap the exposed bones tightly with foil to keep them from charring on the grill. Set aside.

Prepare a medium-low fire in a charcoal grill, or preheat a gas grill on medium-low.

While the grill is preheating, place the cumin in a small saucepan over low heat. Toast the cumin, stirring constantly, to release its fragrance, about 1 minute. Add the barbecue sauce, maple syrup, and chiles and cook, stirring frequently, until hot, bubbly, and slightly thickened, about 3 minutes. Remove from the heat and keep warm while grilling the pork chops.

Brush the grill grate with vegetable oil. Place the chops directly over the fire. Cover the grill and cook the chops on one side for 10 to 12 minutes. Turn the chops, cover again, and cook until the juices run clear and no pink remains when tested with a knife, or an instant-read thermometer registers 160°F, 10 to 12 minutes longer. Brush the pork with the barbecue sauce during the last 1 to 2 minutes of grilling. Serve immediately.

Barbecued Baby Back Ribs

↦ serves 4 to 6

Perfectly smoked and lightly charred baby back ribs are a real treat. To get great results, first make the seasoning rub and coat the ribs with it thoroughly. Next, build a fire using natural lump charcoal (it looks like small hunks of tree limbs) or, as a second choice, "natural" briquettes (without nitrates or petroleum products). Also, consider the types of wood chips you want to use. For example, applewood chips produce a sweet, fragrant smoke, while hickory chips provide a fuller, stronger smoke. Finally, be patient and smoke the ribs slowly over a low fire, adding soaked wood chips frequently to maintain the smoke.

BARBECUE SEASONING RUB

$1/4$ cup sugar

2 tablespoons kosher salt

4 tablespoons paprika

1 tablespoon ground cumin

2 tablespoons chili powder

1 tablespoon freshly ground white pepper

2 tablespoons granulated garlic

1 tablespoon onion powder

$1/4$ teaspoon cayenne pepper

$1/8$ teaspoon ground cloves

4 racks pork baby back ribs
(about $1^1/2$ pounds each), skinned

3 to 4 cups applewood or hickory chips

Vegetable oil for brushing

2 to 3 cups barbecue sauce of choice

To make the Barbecue Seasoning Rub, in a small bowl, stir together the sugar, salt, paprika, cumin, chili powder, white pepper, garlic, onion powder, cayenne, and cloves. Using two thirds of the rub, sprinkle it over both sides of each rack of ribs and rub in lightly. Set aside.

Soak the applewood or hickory chips in cold water to cover for at least 30 minutes. Drain the chips and wrap half of them in heavy-duty aluminum foil, making a sealed pouch that has holes poked in it. Make a second foil pouch with the remaining chips. (If you will be using a gas grill with a smoker box, you can put the chips directly in the box, omitting the foil.)

Meanwhile, set up the grill for indirect cooking. Prepare a medium fire in a charcoal grill, and when the charcoal fire is at the white ash stage, mound the coals against one side of the grill. Or preheat one side of a gas grill. Place a foil pouch of chips over the coals or on the grate of the gas grill. Brush the grill grate with vegetable oil.

Arrange the ribs, meaty-side down, on the side of the grill away from the coals or heat elements. Cover the grill and smoke-cook the ribs for 35 to 45 minutes, tending the fire and keeping the smoke going. At this stage, the object is not to brown the ribs but to smoke them and to cook them until tender and just barely cooked through. Turn the ribs, and add the remaining pouch of wood chips. Cover and grill until the barest amount of pink shows when you cut into the shortest, thickest end of each slab, 35 to 45 minutes longer. The meat should just be starting to pull back, exposing about $1/2$ inch of the rib bones on the thin side of the rib. Transfer the ribs to large, rimmed baking sheets, lay them flat, and set aside while you rebuild the fire.

Rebuild a medium fire, adding more coals and spreading them evenly in the grill. For a gas grill, turn all the burners to medium. Season the ribs again with the remaining rub. Grill the ribs directly over the fire, turning occasionally, until heated through and showing a slight bit of char, about 5 minutes. Brush the ribs with the barbecue sauce just before you take them off the grill.

Transfer the ribs to a carving board, split each rack in half, and cut partially between the bones, leaving the racks intact. Serve immediately or keep warm until serving.

FAVORITE FAMILY MEALS

Roast Chicken
Grand Ma'Mere ↔ serves 4

When visiting friends and staying for several days, I am often encouraged, closer to nudged, to show my "chef stuff" and cook in their kitchen. This is the recipe I often make because it is slightly elegant, while still being approachable, and it is loved for its combination of deeply rich flavors. I have titled this recipe **grand ma'mere,** *or "grandmother style," to emphasize its rustic simplicity. Serve the chicken with mashed potatoes and a colorful vegetable mélange.*

DOUBLE CHICKEN STOCK

2 pounds chicken bones, including backs and necks

2 carrots, peeled and chopped

1 small yellow onion, chopped

2 celery stalks, chopped

1 can (49 ounces) low-sodium chicken broth

ROAST CHICKEN BREASTS

4 whole chicken breasts (11 ounces each), first
wing bone still attached, breastbone removed

Kosher salt

Freshly ground black pepper

3 tablespoons extra-virgin olive oil

To make the Double Chicken Stock, preheat the oven to 425°F. Arrange the chicken bones, carrots, onion, and celery on a rimmed baking sheet and roast until well browned, about 50 minutes. Remove from the oven and pour off all of the grease. Transfer the chicken bones and vegetables to a 4-quart saucepan. While the baking sheet is still warm, pour 1 cup or so of the chicken broth into the baking sheet and, using a spoon, scrape loose all of the brown bits sticking to the pan. Pour this and the balance of the chicken broth into the saucepan.

Place the saucepan over medium heat, bring to a simmer, and cook, uncovered, for 1 hour, skimming off fat with the side of a spoon as it rises to the surface. Pour the stock through a fine-mesh sieve into a clean saucepan and place over medium-low heat. Continue to simmer until reduced by half, about 30 minutes. Set aside. (The stock can be made ahead, covered, and refrigerated for up to 5 days, or frozen for up to 3 months.)

To pan-roast the chicken, preheat the oven to 425°F. Season the chicken breasts on both sides with salt and pepper. In a large, oven-proof skillet over high heat, warm the olive oil. Carefully arrange the chicken breasts, skin-side down, in the pan and cook until the skin is well browned, 6 to 8 minutes. Turn the chicken breasts over and cook

continued

GRAND MA'MERE SAUCE

1 cup coarsely chopped cooked bacon

1 cup roasted garlic cloves (page 14)

1 cup pearl onions, peeled

    (see Cook's Note)

3 cups Double Chicken Stock (page 118), warmed

1 teaspoon chopped fresh thyme

Kosher salt

Freshly ground black pepper

4 tablespoons (1/2 stick) ice-cold unsalted butter,

    cut into small cubes

for 2 minutes on the other side. Place the skillet in the oven and pan-roast the chicken until well browned and the juices run clear when the breast is pierced at the thickest point and the wing bone moves freely, 12 to 14 minutes. Transfer the chicken to warmed dinner plates, tent with aluminum foil, and keep warm. Discard any accumulated grease from the pan.

To make the Grand Ma'Mere Sauce, place the large skillet over medium heat, combine the bacon, roasted garlic, and pearl onions, and cook until the bacon begins to crisp again, 3 to 4 minutes. Add the Double Chicken Stock and, using a wooden spoon, scrape loose all of the brown bits sticking to the pan. Raise the heat to high and bring the stock to a rapid boil. Boil until the stock is reduced by half and the onions are tender, about 10 minutes. Reduce the heat to low, stir in the thyme, and season to taste with salt and pepper. Gradually stir in the butter until it is incorporated.

Spoon one fourth of the sauce over each chicken breast, evenly distributing the bacon, garlic, and pearl onions. Serve immediately.

Cook's Note: *To peel pearl onions easily, cut a shallow "X" in the stem end of each onion, add the onions to boiling water, blanch for 1 minute, drain, and then slip off the skins.*

Bistro Roasted Chicken

↔ serves 4 to 6

One of life's great pleasures is a perfectly roasted chicken, tender and juicy inside, crisp and flavorful on the outside. This recipe is from a restaurant that roasts their chickens in a wood-fired brick oven, with temperatures close to 600°F. If you have a wood-fired oven, by all means cook your chicken in it. Otherwise, roast your chicken in a conventional oven as directed in this recipe. Looking back, I remember that my grandmother cooked everything in and on a wood-burning stove—a cook ahead of her time.

For this recipe, use a free-range chicken, always fresh, never frozen. An ideal accompaniment would be the Rustic Roasted Vegetables (page 154) and Roasted Garlic with Warm Crusty Baguettes (page 14).

1 chicken (about 3^1/$_2$ pounds), trimmed of
    excess fat and halved

Kosher salt

Freshly ground black pepper

^{1}/$_2$ cup extra-virgin olive oil

1 tablespoon chopped fresh rosemary

1 tablespoon chopped fresh thyme

1 tablespoon chopped fresh oregano

3 cloves garlic, minced

Position a rack in the upper third of the oven and preheat to 475°F. Season the cavity of each chicken half with salt and pepper. Place the chicken halves, skin-side up, in a large baking pan. In a small bowl, combine the olive oil, rosemary, thyme, oregano, and garlic and stir until well blended. Spread this mixture all over the skin side of the chicken, and season generously with salt and pepper.

Roast the chicken for 25 minutes. Pour off any accumulated juices and rotate the pan 180 degrees to ensure even browning. Reduce the heat to 375°F and move the chicken to the middle rack of the oven. Continue to roast until the juices run clear when the thigh meat is pierced with a knife, the chicken is almost mahogany in color, and the drumstick moves easily, about 30 minutes longer.

Remove the chicken from the oven and let rest for 5 to 8 minutes before cutting into individual portions and serving.

Chicken Potpie
with Angel Biscuits ↔ serves 6

Old-fashioned comfort foods never go out of style. Certain dishes, especially potpies, evolve ever so slightly with the addition or deletion of certain vegetables yet still remain recognizable, heartwarming, and classic. If you have never made biscuits from scratch, now is the time to try. There is nothing more fun than rolling up your sleeves and "making pat-a-cake" with a batch of dough and your hands covered in flour.

1/2 cup fresh peas or thawed frozen peas

1 cup peeled, thinly sliced carrots

1/2 pound asparagus, tough ends removed and cut
    on the diagonal into 1/2-inch lengths

1 cup broccoli florets

2 tablespoons unsalted butter

1 1/2 pounds boneless, skinless chicken breast,
    cut into 1/2-inch cubes

1 shallot, minced

1/2 cup all-purpose flour

1/2 cup dry white wine

2 cans (14.5 ounces) low-sodium chicken broth

2 cups heavy (whipping) cream

1/2 cup fresh or thawed frozen corn kernels

2 teaspoons chopped fresh flat-leaf parsley

Kosher salt

Freshly ground black pepper

Angel Biscuits dough (page 175), cut into
    3-inch rounds

1 large egg

1 tablespoon water

Bring a large pot of salted water to a boil over high heat. Add the peas and carrots and cook until crisp-tender, 2 to 3 minutes. Using a slotted spoon, transfer the vegetables to a paper towel–lined baking sheet and set aside. Add the asparagus and broccoli to the boiling water and cook until crisp-tender and bright green, about 3 minutes. Using a slotted spoon, transfer the vegetables to the baking sheet. Set aside.

Preheat the oven to 375°F. In a large skillet over medium-high heat, melt the butter. Add the chicken and sauté, stirring frequently, until the chicken is well browned, about 6 minutes. Add the shallot and cook for another minute to soften slightly. Sprinkle the flour over the chicken, reduce the heat to low, and cook, stirring constantly, for 1 minute. Add the wine and cook for 2 minutes. Gradually stir in the chicken broth, whisking to dissolve the flour. Add the cream, bring to a simmer, and cook, stirring occasionally, until the sauce thickens, about 5 minutes. Stir in the carrots, peas, asparagus, broccoli, corn, and parsley. Season to taste with salt and pepper.

Immediately transfer the mixture to a deep-dish 10-inch pie plate and top with the biscuit rounds, or divide among individual ovenproof ramekins and top each with a biscuit.

In a small bowl, whisk together the egg and water. Using a pastry brush, lightly brush the surface of the biscuits with the egg mixture. Bake the potpie until the biscuits are nicely browned and the filling is bubbly hot, 14 to 17 minutes. Serve immediately.

Panfried Chicken Breast
with Oyster Mushrooms and Tarragon ↔ serves 6

In my family, everyone has his or her special birthday request dinner. This is the recipe my son, Philip, asks for every year. I developed the recipe, so, of course, I feel honored and pleased to make this special birthday meal. My wife, Ellen, gets a tad bit upset because Philip has chosen my dish over hers. I've tried to put the right spin on the situation by suggesting that Philip's choice gives Ellen a well-deserved break from kitchen duties—a special day for her, too. –JOHN CLEM

6 boneless, skinless chicken breast halves

1 cup all-purpose flour

$1/3$ cup unseasoned dried bread crumbs

1 teaspoon kosher salt, plus salt to taste

$1/2$ teaspoon freshly ground black pepper, plus
     pepper to taste

1 large egg

$1/2$ cup milk

4 tablespoons olive oil, plus more as needed

1 cup dry white wine

1 can (14.5 ounces) low-sodium chicken broth

$1/2$ cup (1 stick) unsalted butter

$3/4$ pound oyster mushrooms, stems trimmed

1 tablespoon Dijon mustard

$1/2$ teaspoon chopped fresh tarragon

Place the chicken breasts between 2 pieces of plastic wrap and, using the flat side of a meat mallet, pound them lightly until they are quite flat, about $1/4$ inch thick. In a bowl, stir together the flour, bread crumbs, 1 teaspoon salt, and $1/2$ teaspoon pepper. In a small bowl, whisk together the egg and milk. Dip the chicken in the egg wash, making sure it is well coated, and then dredge in the flour mixture, turning to coat both sides thoroughly. Set aside on a baking sheet.

Preheat the oven to 250°F. Heat a large skillet over medium-high heat, add 3 tablespoons of the olive oil and swirl to coat the bottom of the pan. Arrange the chicken, without crowding, in the pan. (You may need to brown the chicken in 2 batches, adding more oil to the pan, if needed.) Cook until golden brown on one side, 3 to 4 minutes. Turn and cook on the other side until nicely browned, about 3 minutes longer. Transfer the chicken to a baking sheet and keep warm in the oven.

Drain any excess oil from the pan and return the pan to high heat. Add $2/3$ cup of the wine and boil, stirring to free up the browned bits from the bottom of the pan, until the wine is reduced to about 2 table-spoons. Add the chicken broth and simmer until reduced to $1/2$ cup, about 5 minutes.

Meanwhile, place a skillet over high heat, add the remaining 1 table-spoon olive oil and 2 tablespoons of the butter and swirl to coat the bottom of the pan. Add the mushrooms and sauté until nicely browned, about 3 minutes. Add the remaining $1/3$ cup wine and simmer until almost evaporated. Season with salt and pepper. Remove from the heat and set aside.

When the chicken broth has reduced to $1/2$ cup, reduce the heat to medium-low and stir in the mustard. Cut the remaining 6 tablespoons butter into small cubes and add the cubes, a few at a time, to the broth, stirring constantly to incorporate them with the reduced liquid. Add the tarragon and season to taste with salt and pepper. Add the mushrooms to the sauce and cook until heated through.

Remove the chicken breasts from the oven and arrange on warmed dinner plates. Divide the mushrooms evenly among the plates, placing them on top of the chicken. Spoon some of the sauce over the chicken and mushrooms and serve immediately.

Vallary-Style Chicken

↔ serves 6

One of the problems with having a chef for a dad is that you can be a little intimidated when it comes to cooking meals. Having taken the challenge, I know that it is really no problem. Any food cooked with respect for the ingredients and for the love of family and friends will always taste better than food served at a restaurant. This is one of the first recipes that I prepared at home for the family. I think I saw my dad peeking over my shoulder but I don't think he was really supervising me! –VALLARY NORTHERN

1 chicken (about 3¹/₂ pounds), trimmed of
    excess fat and cut into 8 pieces
Kosher salt
Freshly ground black pepper
¹/₄ cup extra-virgin olive oil
6 cloves garlic, thinly sliced
1 can (14.5 ounces) low-sodium chicken broth
2 ounces fresh basil sprigs, leaves torn into large
    pieces and stems reserved
3 cans (14.5 ounces each) plum tomatoes
    in juice, drained

Season the chicken on all sides with salt and pepper. In a large, heavy skillet over medium-high heat, warm the olive oil. Arrange the chicken pieces, skin-side down, in the skillet and cook until nicely browned on one side, about 7 minutes. Turn the chicken and cook for 7 minutes longer. Transfer the chicken to a plate and set aside.

Pour off all but 2 tablespoons of the oil in the pan. Place the pan over low heat and add the garlic. Cook, stirring constantly, until the garlic just begins to turn light tan, about 1 minute. Add the chicken broth and basil stems, raise the heat to high, bring to a boil, and boil until the broth is reduced to about ¹/₄ cup. Remove and discard the basil stems.

Return the chicken to the skillet. Break up the tomatoes with the side of the spoon. Smother the chicken with the tomatoes and bring to a simmer. Reduce the heat to low, cover the pan, and simmer until the chicken is tender and nearly falling from the bone, 20 to 30 minutes. Season to taste with salt and pepper.

Just before serving, stir the torn basil leaves into the sauce, then serve immediately.

Chicken Breast Saltimbocca

↦ serves 6

The word Saltimbocca, *Italian for "jump in the mouth," describes the lovely and well-orchestrated flavors of this dish. The prosciutto crisps up just like bacon, while the fresh sage leaf nestled against the chicken delicately perfumes the meat. Make the Double Chicken Stock, it really makes a difference in this recipe. Serve the chicken breasts with a simply prepared seasonal vegetable, such as asparagus in the spring or roasted Brussels sprouts in the fall.*

6 boneless, skinless chicken breast halves,
    tenderloins removed and reserved for
    another use

6 large fresh sage leaves

6 slices prosciutto (1 ounce each)

Kosher salt

Freshly ground black pepper

$1/2$ cup all-purpose flour

3 tablespoons extra-virgin olive oil

1 shallot, minced

$1^{1}/_{2}$ cups dry white wine

1 cup Double Chicken Stock (page 118)

3 tablespoons unsalted butter

Arrange the chicken breasts, smooth-side up and about 3 inches apart, on a long sheet of plastic wrap. Place a sage leaf in the center of each breast, then top each with a prosciutto slice. Lay a long piece of plastic wrap over top and pound the breasts. Remove the plastic wrap, season with salt and pepper, and then carefully dredge each breast in the flour, shaking off the excess.

Preheat the oven to 250°F. In a large skillet over medium-high heat, heat the olive oil and, without crowding the pan, arrange the chicken breasts, prosciutto-side down, in the pan. (You may need to cook them in 2 batches.) Cook until the prosciutto is nicely crisped and the edges of the chicken are golden brown, 4 to 6 minutes. Carefully turn them over, reduce the heat to low, and continue cooking until the chicken is lightly browned but not cooked all the way through, 3 to 4 minutes. Transfer the chicken to a baking sheet and keep warm in the oven.

Drain the oil from the pan, turn the heat to medium and sauté the shallot, stirring constantly, until softened, about 1 minute. Add the wine, stirring to free up the brown bits, and simmer until the wine is almost evaporated. Add the stock and boil until reduced by half, about 6 minutes. Return the chicken to the pan, add the butter, and cook, to coat the chicken and incorporate the butter. Season to taste with salt and pepper. Transfer the chicken to warmed dinner plates, spoon the sauce over the top, dividing evenly, and serve immediately.

Sautéed Chicken Paillard with Angel Hair Pasta ↔ serves 4

A paillard of chicken is simply a chicken breast that has been flattened quite thin by pounding it with a meat mallet. This is done so that the chicken breast cooks quickly, evenly, and remains tender. A famished chef invented this recipe after a busy night of cooking in the restaurant. He put chicken breasts together with some Garlic Tomato Sauce, sautéed fresh spinach and wild mushrooms, and a rosemary-wine butter sauce, and arranged it all over a bed of angel hair pasta. No need for multiple courses—this was a meal on a plate.

4 boneless, skinless chicken breast halves
    (about 6 ounces each)

$1/2$ cup all-purpose flour

1 teaspoon kosher salt

$1/2$ teaspoon freshly ground black pepper

WHITE WINE–BUTTER SAUCE

2 shallots, thinly sliced

2 cups dry white wine

3 tablespoons heavy (whipping) cream

4 fresh thyme sprigs

1 bay leaf

4 black peppercorns

$1/2$ cup (1 stick) ice-cold unsalted butter,
    cut into small cubes

1 teaspoon chopped fresh rosemary

1 tablespoon roasted garlic (page 14)

Kosher salt

Freshly ground black pepper

Place the chicken breasts between 2 pieces of plastic wrap and, using the flat side of a meat mallet, pound them lightly until they are quite flat, about $1/4$ inch thick. On a plate, stir together the flour, salt, and pepper. Dredge the chicken, 1 piece at a time, in the flour mixture, pressing down on it lightly to coat evenly. Transfer to a rimmed baking sheet, cover, and refrigerate until ready to sauté.

To make the White Wine–Butter Sauce, in a small saucepan over medium-high heat, combine the shallots, wine, cream, thyme, bay leaf, and peppercorns. Bring to a simmer and cook, uncovered, until reduced to about $1/4$ cup, 12 to 14 minutes. Strain the mixture through a fine-mesh sieve, reserving the liquid. Return the liquid to the pan, place over low heat, and gradually stir in the cold butter, adding only a couple of cubes at a time while stirring constantly. When all of the butter is incorporated, add the rosemary and roasted garlic and season generously with salt and pepper. (This sauce needs to be well seasoned in order to stand up to the bold flavors of the tomato sauce.) Set aside and keep warm, but not over direct heat.

continued

1 tablespoon kosher salt, plus salt to taste

¾ pound angel-hair pasta

4 tablespoons extra-virgin olive oil

¼ pound oyster mushrooms, stems trimmed

3 ounces spinach, tough stems removed

1½ cups Garlic Tomato Sauce (page 75)

Freshly ground black pepper

1 lemon, cut into wedges

4 fresh rosemary sprigs

Fill an 8- to 10-quart stockpot two-thirds full of water and bring to a boil over high heat. Add 1 tablespoon salt to the boiling water, and then add the pasta. Stir and cook the pasta until al dente (cooked through, but still slightly chewy), 6 to 8 minutes.

To sauté the chicken *paillards,* while the pasta is cooking, in a large skillet over medium-high heat, heat 3 tablespoons of the olive oil and swirl to coat the bottom of the pan. Add the chicken breasts and sauté until lightly browned on one side, 2 to 3 minutes. Turn the chicken over, add the mushrooms to the pan, and sauté the mushrooms while the chicken cooks, about 2 minutes. Add the spinach and the Garlic Tomato Sauce, smothering the chicken and mushrooms with the sauce. Cook until the spinach is wilted but still bright green and the sauce is heated through, 2 to 3 minutes. Season to taste with salt and pepper.

To assemble the dish, drain the pasta in a colander, but do not rinse it, return it to the pasta cooking pot. Toss the pasta with the remaining 1 tablespoon olive oil. Season to taste with salt and pepper. Arrange the pasta off to one side in warmed pasta bowls. Transfer 1 chicken breast to each bowl, leaning the chicken on the pasta. Using a serving spoon, lay a stripe of the tomato-mushroom-spinach sauce across some of the pasta and some of the chicken. Spoon some of the White Wine–Butter Sauce into an open space in the bowls. Garnish each serving with a wedge of lemon and a sprig of rosemary.

Grand Marnier Roasted Chicken

↦ serves 4 to 6

Roasted chicken is arguably the perfect family food. This recipe, an old family favorite, dresses up the bird with a Grand Marnier glaze flavored with grainy mustard, apricot preserves, honey, and, of course, orange liqueur. Easy and quick enough to serve as a weeknight meal, this chicken has just that proper touch of elegance for entertaining as well.
—MOLLY NORDSTROM

1 chicken (about 3^1/$_2$ pounds), trimmed of
   excess fat

1 orange, quartered and seeds removed

3 large fresh rosemary sprigs

1 small yellow onion, quartered

Kosher salt

Freshly ground white pepper

^{1}/$_2$ cup water

3 tablespoons unsalted butter

3 tablespoons whole-grain mustard

3 tablespoons apricot preserves

3 tablespoons honey

3 tablespoons Grand Marnier

Preheat the oven to 400°F. Place the chicken, breast-side up, on a rack in a small roasting pan and squeeze the juice from the orange quarters over the chicken. Place the orange quarters inside the cavity along with the rosemary and onion. Season the chicken generously with salt and pepper. Pour the water into the bottom of the pan.

Roast the chicken for 30 minutes. Rotate the pan 180 degrees and reduce the heat to 375°F. Continue to roast the chicken for 25 minutes longer.

While the chicken is roasting, in a small saucepan over medium-high heat, melt the butter and then stir in the mustard, apricot preserves, and honey. Cook, stirring constantly, until well blended, 2 to 3 minutes. Add the Grand Marnier, stir to blend, and then remove from the heat.

Remove the chicken from the oven, pour off the juices from the pan, and brush the chicken with the Grand Marnier glaze. Continue roasting the chicken, basting frequently with the glaze, until the juices run clear when the thigh meat is pierced with a knife and the drumstick moves easily, about 15 minutes longer. (If the chicken is browning too quickly, tent it with aluminum foil until it is done.)

Remove the chicken from the oven and let rest for about 10 minutes before carving and serving.

Pan-Asian Salmon Baked in Parchment ↔ serves 6

This dish is surprisingly easy to prepare. The parchment paper locks in the moisture and flavor, resulting in a very tender fish. Wild rice or a light pasta dish is a great accompaniment. Combine any leftovers with fresh salad greens for a gourmet main-course salad. –ALICE AND RUSSELL DORR

1 salmon fillet (2 pounds), skin on

1 1/2 teaspoons Asian sesame oil

1 1/2 teaspoons peeled and grated fresh ginger

1 large clove garlic, minced

1/2 yellow onion, cut into paper-thin slices

1 tomato, cored and thinly sliced

1 tablespoon tamari sauce or soy sauce

Kosher salt

Freshly ground black pepper

8 fresh cilantro sprigs

Preheat the oven to 450°F.

Measure the salmon fillet, both its length and its thickness at its thickest point. Cut a piece of parchment paper two times the length of the salmon fillet, plus a few more inches. Fold the parchment in half, crease it, and then unfold it. Place the parchment lengthwise on a large, rimmed baking sheet, the creased edge at one side of the pan and the rest overhanging the pan. Center the salmon fillet on the parchment. If the fillet has a thin side, fold it under itself (so it will cook evenly with the thicker side). Rub the sesame oil over the salmon, then sprinkle the ginger and garlic over it. Arrange the onion slices and tomato slices slightly overlapping on top and drizzle with the tamari or soy sauce. Season lightly with salt and pepper and then arrange the cilantro sprigs on top. Fold the parchment paper over the top of the salmon. Beginning at the corner of one of the open edges, tightly fold about 1/2 inch of the parchment onto itself to crimp the two pieces together, working your way around the paper. The salmon will be completely enclosed and sealed in a pouchlike pocket, which will keep the juices in while the salmon bakes.

Bake the salmon for 10 minutes for each inch of thickness of the fillet. To serve, using 2 long spatulas, transfer the salmon, still in the parchment, to a warmed platter. Present the parchment-enclosed salmon at the table, and then use a knife to slit the parchment open. Cut into portions and serve on warmed plates, spooning the juices over the salmon.

COOK'S NOTE: *The quantities of the flavoring in this recipe can be adjusted up or down to suit your taste. For example, if you love garlic, add more; if you don't, leave it out.*

Oven-Roasted Salmon

↔ serves 6

Have you ever invited guests to dinner on a weeknight and then it turns out your day is so busy that you don't know how you will get everything done? Here's the rescue recipe. The whole side of salmon is roasted intact. As a result, it comes out so tender that it melts in your mouth. Serve the fish on a long platter, surround it with some roasted baby potatoes, steam a vegetable, and, voilà, dinner is made. Any leftovers can be turned into a fantastic salmon salad.

1 salmon fillet (2^1/$_2$ pounds), skin on

3 cloves garlic, minced

2 teaspoons finely chopped fresh rosemary

1 teaspoon freshly chopped fresh thyme

Kosher salt

Freshly ground black pepper

2 tablespoons extra-virgin olive oil

Position a rack in the upper two thirds of the oven and preheat to 450°F. Line a large, rimmed baking sheet with aluminum foil. Place the salmon, skin-side down, in the pan. Rub the garlic all over the flesh side of the salmon, sprinkle with the rosemary and thyme, and then season with salt and pepper. Drizzle with the olive oil.

Roast the salmon for 14 to 20 minutes, depending on the thickness of the fish. The salmon is done when the thickest part of the fillet flakes easily when tested with a fork, or an instant-read thermometer registers 140°F when inserted into the thickest part of the fillet. Serve immediately.

Seafood Baked in Parchment with Spaghettini ↝ serves 8

This recipe features a variety of seafood and shellfish baked in parchment—think of it as an elegant clambake. To bring a little drama to the presentation, serve each parchment packet sealed then, when all the guests have been served, have them all slit open their packets at the same time. The steam will escape and an incredible fragrance will perfume the room. You can almost taste the sea.

1 tablespoon kosher salt, plus salt to taste

1 pound spaghettini

3 1/2 tablespoons extra-virgin olive oil

Freshly ground black pepper

3 cloves garlic; 2 cloves minced, 1 clove halved

1/2 teaspoon red pepper flakes

1 1/2 cups dry white wine

1 pound mussels, well scrubbed and debearded

1 pound clams, well scrubbed

3/4 pound large shrimp, peeled and deveined, with tail segments intact

1 bottle (8 ounces) clam juice

6 tablespoons (3/4 stick) unsalted butter, at room temperature, cut into small cubes

3 cups Garlic Tomato Sauce (page 75)

2 tablespoons chopped fresh basil

Fill an 8- to 10-quart stockpot two-thirds full of water and bring to a boil over high heat. Add 1 tablespoon salt to the boiling water and then add the pasta. Stir and cook the pasta until al dente (cooked through but still slightly chewy), about 8 minutes. Drain the pasta in a colander, rinse with cold water, and drain well. Place the pasta in a bowl and toss with 1 1/2 tablespoons of the olive oil. Season to taste with salt and pepper. Cover and set aside.

To cook the seafood, using a large sauté pan with a tight-fitting lid over medium heat, warm the remaining 2 tablespoons olive oil. Add the minced garlic and red pepper flakes and sauté just until fragrant, about 1 minute. Add the wine and raise the heat to high. Add the mussels, discarding any that fail to close to the touch, cover the pan, and cook until the mussels open, about 2 minutes. Using a slotted spoon, transfer the mussels to a rimmed baking sheet, discarding any that failed to open. Add the clams to the pan, discarding any that fail to close to the touch, cover, and cook just until they open, 1 to 2 minutes depending on their size. Using the slotted spoon, transfer the clams to the baking sheet, discarding any that failed to open. Add the shrimp to the pan, cover, and cook just until they begin to turn pink, about 2 minutes. Using the slotted spoon, transfer the shrimp to the baking sheet. Leave the cooked mussels and clams in their shells. Refrigerate the cooked seafood until you assemble the packets.

Add the clam juice to the combined liquids remaining in the pan and simmer over medium-high heat until reduced to $1/4$ cup, about 10 minutes. Remove from the heat and set aside until the liquid cools to room temperature. Mix in the butter until well blended. Set aside.

Preheat the oven to 400°F. Cut out 6 pieces of parchment paper, each 24 by 12 inches. Fold each sheet in half to form a 12-inch square. Lift the top and rub the bottom portion of each square with the halved garlic clove. Divide the pasta evenly among the parchment squares. Divide the mussels, clams, and shrimp into 6 equal portions and arrange on top of the pasta. Dot each packet with small dabs of the butter mixture, about 1 tablespoon per packet. Spoon $1/2$ cup of the Garlic Tomato Sauce over the seafood in each packet. Season each packet with a little salt and pepper and then sprinkle with the basil. Working with 1 packet at a time, fold the top piece of parchment over and, beginning at one corner, tightly fold about $1/2$ inch of the parchment onto itself, working your way around the packet. You want to create a tight, secure fold all around to trap the juices. Use a wide spatula to transfer the packets to baking sheets.

About 15 minutes before serving, bake the packets until the parchment puffs and the pasta and seafood are completely heated through, 12 to 15 minutes. Use the wide spatula to transfer each packet to a warmed dinner plate and serve immediately.

New Orleans Spicy Cajun Shrimp

↦ serves 6

My grandfather loved southern Louisiana. His interest in gourmet cooking and the sights and sounds of the French Quarter in New Orleans kept him going back even though it was an eight–hour drive from his home in Dallas. One summer, he took my sister and me along. We fell in love with southern Louisiana, ate our way through New Orleans, and loved all the food, too. My grandfather came home with this recipe for spicy Cajun shrimp, and I have been making it ever since.

This is a wonderfully messy dish. Lay newspapers all over the table, have stacks of napkins, and provide several loaves of warm, crusty French bread. The bread is ideal for mopping up the flavorful peppery butter sauce. –EMILY LAWSON

CREOLE SEASONING

1 tablespoon kosher salt

1 teaspoon freshly ground black pepper

1/2 teaspoon cayenne pepper

1 teaspoon dried thyme

1 teaspoon dried oregano

2 teaspoons paprika

2 teaspoons granulated garlic

1 tablespoon granulated onion

CAJUN SHRIMP BUTTER

3/4 pound (3 sticks) unsalted butter,
   at room temperature

2 tablespoons Creole Seasoning (above)

3 cloves garlic, minced

1 tablespoon freshly ground black pepper

1 tablespoon paprika

1 tablespoon granulated onion

1 teaspoon kosher salt

1 tablespoon Worcestershire sauce

1 teaspoon Tabasco sauce

2 pounds large shrimp in the shell, deveined

To make the Creole Seasoning, in a small bowl, combine the salt, black pepper, cayenne, thyme, oregano, paprika, and the granulated garlic and onion. Mix well and store in a jar with a tight-fitting lid.

To make the Cajun Shrimp Butter, in a food processor fitted with the metal blade, combine the butter, Creole Seasoning, garlic, pepper, paprika, granulated onion, salt, Worcestershire sauce, and Tabasco sauce. Process until thoroughly blended. Set aside.

To cook the shrimp, preheat the oven to 450°F. Arrange the shrimp in a 9-by-13-inch baking dish and cover with the Cajun Shrimp Butter.

Bake the shrimp, uncovered, for 10 minutes. Stir the shrimp around and continue baking until the shrimp turn uniformly pink and all the translucence is gone from the thickest part of the bodies, about 2 minutes longer.

Transfer the shrimp and all the butter sauce to a warmed serving dish. Serve immediately.

Tempura Vegetables and Lobster
with Cilantro-Lemongrass Sauce ↦ serves 8 to 10

On a fairly regular basis, my family and friends gather in the kitchen and enjoy tempura vegetables. Everyone stands around the little fryer as each batch of crisp vegetables is lifted from the oil. Pieces are doled out, dipped in sauce, and eaten hot. This is casual entertaining at its best, or just plain family fun.

SOY DIPPING SAUCE

1/4 cup soy sauce

1/4 cup water

1 teaspoon peeled and grated fresh ginger

1 clove garlic, minced

1 tablespoon rice wine vinegar

1 teaspoon sugar

CILANTRO-LEMONGRASS DIPPING SAUCE

2 tablespoons canola oil

1 lemongrass stalk, tender inner bulb only, minced

1 shallot, minced

1 tablespoon peeled and minced fresh ginger

3 tablespoons sugar

1/4 teaspoon kosher salt

2 tablespoons Chinese chile sauce with garlic
(see Cook's Note, page 91)

1 cup rice wine vinegar

3/4 cup water

1/2 bunch fresh cilantro, chopped

BATTER

2 large egg yolks

2 cups ice water

2 1/4 cups all-purpose flour

1 tablespoon cornstarch

Kosher salt

1 tablespoon canola oil

To make the Soy Dipping Sauce, in a small bowl, combine the soy sauce, water, ginger, garlic, vinegar, and sugar. Mix until the sugar dissolves. Set aside.

To make the Cilantro-Lemongrass Dipping Sauce, in a small saucepan over low heat, warm the canola oil. Add the lemongrass, shallot, and ginger and sauté, stirring constantly, just until fragrant, about 1 minute. Add the sugar, salt, and chile sauce with garlic and cook, stirring constantly, until the sugar is dissolved, about 2 minutes. Add the vinegar and water, bring to a simmer, and cook the sauce for 2 to 3 minutes. Set aside to cool to room temperature, then stir in the cilantro.

To make the batter, in a large bowl, whisk together the egg yolks and ice water, and then gradually add the flour and cornstarch. The batter should have a few small lumps in it and be a little thinner than pancake batter. Season with a little salt and stir in the canola oil. Set aside.

To make the tempura, pour the canola oil to a depth of at least 3 inches in a large, deep saucepan or wok. Place over medium-high heat and heat to 375ºF on a deep-frying thermometer.

continued

About 6 cups canola oil for deep-frying

1 sweet potato, peeled and cut into
$1/8$-inch-thick rounds

1 Idaho potato, peeled and cut into
$1/4$-inch-thick rounds

$1/2$ pound asparagus, tough ends removed and
cut on the diagonal into 2-inch lengths

1 handful snow peas, stems and strings removed

2 yellow bell peppers, seeded, deribbed, and
cut into $1/4$-inch-wide rings

2 red bell peppers, seeded, deribbed, and cut
into $1/4$-inch-wide rings

2 carrots, peeled and cut into 2-inch-long
matchsticks

2 small zucchini, ends trimmed, cut in half
lengthwise, seeds removed, and cut into
thick matchsticks

$1/2$ pound button mushrooms, stems trimmed
and quartered

$1/2$ pound green beans, trimmed, cooked just until
crisp-tender, chilled, and patted dry

1 yellow onion, cut crosswise into $1/2$-inch-thick
rings

All-purpose flour for dusting

Kosher salt

2 lobster tails (about 1 pound total), shells
removed, deveined, halved lengthwise, and
then cut crosswise into thin slices

While the oil is heating, place some of the vegetables in a large bowl. Toss lightly with flour. Taking a handful at a time, dip the vegetables in the tempura batter, lift them out, and then carefully place them in the oil. It is important to fry the vegetables in small batches to maintain the temperature of the oil. Using a slotted spoon or wire skimmer, turn the vegetables occasionally and fry them until they rise to the surface and are crisp and lightly browned, about 2 minutes. Using the spoon or skimmer, transfer the vegetables to a paper towel–lined baking sheet and sprinkle lightly with salt. Continue frying until all the vegetables are cooked, always being sure the oil is at 375°F before adding the next batch. When all the vegetables are fried, toss the lobster slices lightly in flour, coat with the tempura batter, and fry just until cooked through and the batter is crisp and lightly browned, about $1 1/2$ minutes. Using the slotted spoon or wire skimmer, transfer to the baking sheet to drain briefly.

Arrange the tempura on warmed dinner plates or on a large serving platter. Pass the Soy Dipping Sauce and the Cilantro-Lemongrass Dipping Sauce. Serve immediately.

Veal Meat Loaf
with Shiitake Mushroom Gravy ↦ serves 6 to 8

This is an elegant version of a classic comfort food dish, making it suitable for serving at even the most special dinner celebrations. Although the meat loaf can be prepared in a loaf pan, making it free-form on a rimmed baking sheet produces better results. The loaf browns on all sides, the fat runs off, and the meat remains tender. Roasted Garlic Mashed Potatoes (page 163) are a perfect companion.

$^1/_2$ cup unseasoned fresh bread crumbs

$^1/_2$ cup milk

1 tablespoon olive oil

$^1/_2$ cup minced leek, white and light green part only

2 pounds ground veal

1 large egg, lightly beaten

$^1/_2$ cup (2 ounces) freshly grated Parmesan cheese

3 slices bacon, fried until crisp and finely chopped

1 small yellow onion, minced

1 teaspoon minced fresh sage

Kosher salt

Freshly ground black pepper

MUSHROOM GRAVY

3 tablespoons extra-virgin olive oil

2 cloves garlic, minced

2 cups sliced shiitake mushroom caps

4 cups heavy (whipping) cream

$^1/_2$ cup (2 ounces) freshly grated Parmesan cheese

Kosher salt

Freshly ground black pepper

Preheat the oven to 325°F. In a small bowl, soak the bread crumbs in the milk until the milk is absorbed, about 5 minutes. In a small sauté pan over medium heat, warm the oil and swirl to coat the bottom of the pan. Add the leek and sauté until softened but not brown, about 3 minutes. Set aside.

In a large bowl, combine the veal, soaked bread crumbs, leek, egg, Parmesan, bacon, onion, and sage. Mix together to distribute the ingredients evenly. Season with salt and pepper. Press the meat mixture together, transfer to the center of a large baking dish or rimmed baking sheet, and form into an oval log.

Bake the meat loaf until it is lightly browned and an instant-read thermometer inserted into the middle registers 160°F, 45 to 60 minutes.

Meanwhile, make the Mushroom Gravy. In a sauté pan or skillet over low heat, warm the oil and swirl to coat the bottom of the pan. Add the garlic and sauté, stirring constantly, until it is light tan, about 1 minute. Add the mushrooms, increase the heat to medium, and sauté, stirring occasionally, until the mushrooms begin to brown, about 3 minutes. Add the cream and simmer until the cream reduces by half, about 8 minutes. Remove from the heat and stir in the Parmesan. The sauce should be thick enough to coat the back of a spoon. Season to taste with salt and pepper. Set aside and keep warm.

Cut the meat loaf into thick slices and transfer to warmed dinner plates. Top each serving with some of the gravy and serve immediately.

Panfried Veal with Arugula Salad ↳ serves 4

I assumed most veal dishes were served with heavy sauces, laden with calories, until I ate an Italian veal dish in Milan. The dish was prepared with a bone–in veal chop that had been pounded quite flat. It was an impressive presentation topped with a light and refreshing arugula salad. Trying to be more economical, I use veal scallopini in this recipe. However, the arugula salad is just as I remember in Italy, colorful, brilliantly flavored, and a perfect complement to the veal.

1^1/$_4$ pounds thinly sliced veal, from the leg
   (scallopini)

1 cup all-purpose flour

Kosher salt

Freshly ground black pepper

2 large eggs

1 cup or more unseasoned dried bread crumbs

^{1}/$_4$ cup olive oil, plus more as needed

^{1}/$_2$ pound arugula, stems removed

4 plum tomatoes, cored, halved, and cut
   crosswise into thin slices

^{1}/$_4$ red onion, thinly sliced

^{1}/$_3$ cup extra-virgin olive oil

2 tablespoons balsamic vinegar

4 lemon wedges

When purchased, the veal cutlets should be less than ^{1}/$_4$ inch thick; if they are not, place them between 2 sheets of plastic wrap and pound them gently with the flat side of a meat mallet to a uniform thickness.

Organize the 3 coatings. Place the flour on a dinner plate and season generously with salt and pepper. In a shallow, wide bowl, beat the eggs together; set next to the flour. Place the bread crumbs on a dinner plate and set the plate next to the eggs. Have a baking sheet ready. Dredge the cutlets, one at a time, in the flour, shaking off the excess. Then dip them in the egg and let the excess drain off. Finally, coat lightly but completely with the bread crumbs. Place the cutlets on the baking sheet until ready to sauté. Preheat the oven to 200°F.

In a large skillet over medium-high heat, warm the ^{1}/$_4$ cup olive oil and swirl to coat the bottom of the pan. The oil is properly heated when a tiny pinch of flour sizzles on contact. Working in batches, add the cutlets to the pan without crowding, adjust the heat so the oil bubbles around the veal, and sauté until the cutlets are nicely browned on one side, about 2 minutes. Turn the cutlets and cook the other side until golden and the coating looks crisp, about 2 minutes longer. Remove from the skillet and hold on an ovenproof platter in the warm oven. Repeat until the cutlets are cooked, adding more oil if needed.

In a large bowl, combine the arugula, tomatoes, and onion. Drizzle with the extra-virgin olive oil and the vinegar and season lightly with salt and pepper. Toss until evenly coated. Transfer the veal cutlets to warmed plates, top with the arugula salad, and garnish with the lemon wedges. Serve immediately.

Korean-Style Fire Beef
in Crisp Lettuce Cups → serves 4

Korean bul go gi *is often translated as "fire beef." This version serves the sizzling-hot beef in cool and refreshing iceberg lettuce cups. The contrast of textures, temperatures, and flavors is simply delightful. Serve with kimchi, which can be found at Asian markets or in the Asian-food section of well-stocked supermarkets.* —DAVID KIM

1 pound beef sirloin, sliced across the grain
    about ¹/₈ inch thick

1 tablespoon sugar

2 tablespoons sake

2¹/₂ tablespoons soy sauce

1 tablespoon Asian sesame oil

2 cloves garlic, finely minced

1¹/₂ teaspoons peeled and minced fresh ginger

¹/₄ cup chopped green onion, white and light green
    part only

2 teaspoons sesame seeds, toasted
    (see Cook's Note, page 190)

1 tablespoon water

1 teaspoon freshly ground black pepper

1 head iceberg lettuce

1 tablespoon vegetable oil

Kimchi for serving (optional)

Place the beef slices in a large, shallow baking dish. Sprinkle them with the sugar and drizzle with 1 tablespoon of the sake. Set aside at room temperature while preparing the marinade.

In a small bowl, combine the remaining 1 tablespoon sake, the soy sauce, sesame oil, garlic, ginger, green onion, sesame seeds, water, and pepper. Whisk together and pour over the beef, making sure the beef is completely immersed in the marinade. Cover and marinate overnight in the refrigerator.

Core the head of lettuce and then peel off whole leaves from it. You will need 12 cup-shaped leaves. Rinse the leaves well under cool water and drain upside down on a rimmed baking sheet lined with a double thickness of paper towels. Refrigerate until ready to serve. Reserve the remaining lettuce for another use.

To cook the beef, remove it from the marinade. Heat a well-seasoned, large cast-iron skillet over medium-high heat. Add the vegetable oil and swirl to coat the bottom of the pan. Add the beef, working in batches if necessary to avoid crowding, and sauté, turning and moving the slices as they cook, until cooked through, 3 to 4 minutes. Remove from the heat.

For each serving, arrange some of the beef on one side of a warmed dinner plate and place a lettuce cup on the other side. Pass the extra beef and lettuce cups separately. Show your family and friends how to fill the lettuce cups with the beef and then a little of the kimchi, if desired, and eat out of hand.

Cassoulet

↦ serves 10 to 12

Cassoulet, a traditional French country dish, is perfect for fall and winter entertaining because you can feed a hungry group of friends and family with the majority of the work completed in advance. Although it is basically a combination of tender meats and poultry stewed with beans, cassoulet can range from the most basic to the very complicated and grand. This recipe falls comfortably in between. The Roasted Garlic with Warm Crusty Baguettes (page 14) and a simple green salad make a wonderful accompaniment to this classic French recipe. –CHEF DAVID SHAW

$^3/_4$ pound boneless pork shoulder, cut into
 $1^1/_2$-inch cubes

$^3/_4$ pound boneless lamb shoulder, cut into
 $1^1/_2$-inch cubes

1 pound mild Italian garlic sausage, cut into
 2-inch pieces

4 chicken thighs

5 tablespoons olive oil

$^1/_4$ teaspoon kosher salt, plus salt to taste

Freshly ground black pepper

$1^1/_2$ cups red wine

1 can (14.5 ounces) low-sodium beef broth

1 cup slab bacon ($^1/_2$-inch dice)

1 cup chopped yellow onion

$1^1/_2$ cups chopped, peeled carrot

1 large fennel bulb, tops removed, halved
 lengthwise, cored, and thinly sliced crosswise

4 cloves garlic, minced

1 bay leaf

1 teaspoon dried thyme

1 can (6 ounces) tomato paste

$^1/_2$ cup ketchup

Preheat the oven to 350°F. Arrange the pork, lamb, sausage, and chicken in a large roasting pan or on a rimmed baking sheet large enough to spread out the meat without crowding. Drizzle 4 tablespoons of the olive oil over the meats, season with salt and pepper, and then toss to coat the meats evenly. Roast the meats until they are tender and brown, 50 to 60 minutes. Remove from the oven, transfer the meat to a large plate or baking dish, and set aside.

Drain off any accumulated fat from the pan and discard. While the pan is still warm, add the wine and beef broth. Using the back of a wooden spoon, stir to free up the browned bits from the bottom of the pan. Pour the wine mixture into a separate container and set aside.

In a heavy, 3-quart saucepan over medium heat, cook the bacon, stirring frequently, until well browned and the fat is rendered, 10 to 12 minutes. Pour off all but 3 tablespoons of the fat. Add the onion, carrot, and fennel to the pan and sauté stirring frequently, until the vegetables are lightly browned and softened, 8 to 10 minutes. Add three fourths of the garlic, the bay leaf, and the thyme and sauté for 2 minutes longer. Add the wine mixture and simmer until reduced by one third, about 8 minutes. Stir in the tomato paste and ketchup. Add the beans, reduce the heat to low, and simmer, stirring frequently, until some of the liquid is absorbed and the mixture is no longer soupy, about 10 minutes.

4 cans (15 ounces each) Great Northern beans,
   drained and rinsed
$1/4$ cup unseasoned dried bread crumbs
Sour cream for garnish

Transfer the bean mixture to an attractive 8-quart oven-to-table baking dish. Arrange the roasted meats on top and press them into the beans. Cover the casserole and bake at 350°F until the meat is fork-tender, about 1 hour.

Meanwhile, in a small bowl, combine the bread crumbs, the $1/4$ teaspoon salt, the remaining 1 tablespoon olive oil, and the remaining minced garlic. When the meat is tender, remove the baking dish from the oven and increase the oven temperature to 425°F. Sprinkle the bread crumb mixture evenly over the surface and return the dish to the oven. Bake, uncovered, until the bread crumbs are nicely browned, 10 to 15 minutes. Serve with sour cream for spooning on top.

Grandmother's Spring Leg of Lamb with Honey-Glazed Carrots and Parsleyed New Potatoes ↪ *serves 8 to 10*

One of my fondest childhood memories is of my grandmother's cooking. She made cooking incredibly fun; we all got to help in the planning, preparation, and serving of the meal. I think this is one of the reasons I became a chef. Her philosophy of food and cooking—let the ingredients speak for themselves—was something I have carried into my professional life. She always bought only the freshest seasonal ingredients and prepared them simply. This recipe of hers, a family treasure, reflects that style. Once a year the butcher would get fresh spring lamb, and she would be the first in line to pick out a leg. –MICHAEL THOMS

1 leg of lamb (about 4 pounds), boned, rolled, and tied

8 cloves garlic, quartered

$1/4$ cup fresh rosemary leaves

4 teaspoons kosher salt, plus salt to taste

Freshly ground black pepper

2 pounds baby red potatoes

$1^1/2$ pounds baby bunch carrots, peeled and trimmed, with $1/2$ inch of green tops intact

Ice water

$1^1/4$ cups ($2^1/2$ sticks) unsalted butter

2 tablespoons chopped fresh flat-leaf parsley

$1/4$ cup firmly packed light brown sugar

$1/2$ cup honey

Preheat the oven to 425°F. Use a small paring knife to cut small slits all around the exterior of the lamb roast. Insert a piece of garlic and a few rosemary leaves into each incision. Season the roast well, rubbing in a generous amount of salt and pepper. Place the lamb on a rack in a roasting pan.

Roast the lamb for 20 minutes to sear it. Reduce the oven temperature to 350°F and continue roasting until the meat registers done when pierced in the thickest portion with an instant-read thermometer, 20 to 40 minutes longer, depending on desired doneness. The internal temperature for rare lamb is 125°F, for medium-rare 130°F, for medium 140°F, and for well-done 150°F. Start testing for rare lamb after 40 minutes; well-done meat may take up to $1^1/4$ hours. Allow the roast to rest for 10 to 15 minutes before carving.

While the lamb is roasting, cook the potatoes. In a large saucepan, combine the potatoes with water to cover by at least 2 inches. Place over high heat and bring to a boil. Add 1 tablespoon salt, partially cover the pan, reduce the heat, and simmer until tender when pierced with a paring knife, 20 to 30 minutes. Drain the potatoes and set aside.

Bring another saucepan of water to a boil and add 1 teaspoon salt. Add the carrots and cook until tender with a touch of "snap" remaining, 2 to 4 minutes, depending on their size. Using a slotted spoon, transfer the carrots to a bowl of ice water, immersing them completely for 1 minute. Drain well, then place on a plate lined with a double thickness of paper towels to absorb moisture. Set aside.

While the meat is resting, finish the potatoes and carrots. In the same saucepan that was used to cook the potatoes, melt $^3/_4$ cup of the butter over medium-high heat. Add the potatoes and parsley and toss with the butter. Season to taste with salt and pepper. Cover and keep warm.

In a large skillet over medium-high heat, melt the remaining $^1/_2$ cup butter. Add the carrots and cook, stirring frequently, until just beginning to glaze and show a touch of brown, 4 to 5 minutes. Reduce the heat to low, sprinkle the carrots with the sugar, and drizzle with the honey. Cook, stirring constantly, until the carrots are candied, about 2 minutes. Season to taste with salt and pepper. Keep warm.

To serve, snip the strings on the roast and slice the lamb into $^1/_4$-inch-thick slices. Arrange overlapping slices on a large, warmed serving platter. Scatter the potatoes and carrots around the rim of the platter and serve immediately.

Macadamia-and-Honey-Crusted
Rack of Lamb ↔ serves 4

I consider American lamb the finest you can buy. Each rack of lamb consists of seven bones, so you will need two racks to serve four people. Ask your butcher to french the racks, which involves cutting away the meat and fat from the ends of the ribs and removing the chine bone so that the rack can be easily carved at the table. Serve the lamb with a seasonal vegetable and with Gruyère and Custard Baked Potatoes (page 164), whose rich taste and aroma is the ideal complement. Plan ahead, as the lamb needs to marinate overnight. –JEFF BARKWILL

MUSTARD-ROSEMARY MARINADE

3/4 cup dry white wine

2 tablespoons chopped fresh rosemary

4 cloves garlic, minced

2 tablespoons Dijon mustard

1 tablespoon extra-virgin olive oil

1/2 teaspoon kosher salt

1/4 teaspoon freshly ground black pepper

2 racks of lamb (about 1 1/2 pounds each), frenched (see recipe introduction)

MACADAMIA CRUST

1/4 cup chopped fresh flat-leaf parsley

1/2 cup finely chopped macadamia nuts

1/2 cup unseasoned dried bread crumbs

1/4 cup honey

To make the Mustard-Rosemary Marinade, in a small, nonreactive saucepan over medium-high heat, combine the wine, rosemary, garlic, mustard, oil, salt, and pepper. Bring to a simmer and cook until reduced by half, about 10 minutes. Remove from the heat and let cool to room temperature. Place the lamb racks in a 1-gallon lock-top plastic bag and pour the marinade over them. Squeeze all the air out of the bag, seal, place in a baking dish, and allow the lamb to marinate overnight or for up to 24 hours before roasting.

Position a rack in the upper two thirds of the oven and preheat to 400°F.

To make the Macadamia Crust, in a small bowl, stir together the parsley, nuts, and bread crumbs. Remove the lamb from the marinade and pat very dry with paper towels so that the crust will adhere well. Pour the honey over the lamb racks, avoiding the bones, and use your fingers to spread the honey evenly. Using the palm of your hand and applying a slight amount of pressure, press the nut mixture over the meat. Cover the exposed rib bones with aluminum foil to keep them from burning and then place the lamb racks in a shallow roasting pan.

Roast the lamb racks until an instant-read thermometer inserted into the thickest part of the lamb registers 125°F for medium-rare, about 30 minutes. Roast longer if you prefer. Remove the racks from the oven and let rest for 5 minutes. To carve, separate the ribs by cutting between the bones. Serve immediately.

Winter Pot Roast with Baby Carrots and Potatoes ↔ serves 8

Here's a venerable wintertime dish that won't keep you chained to the kitchen all day. Make it on a day when you're hanging around the house, catching up at your desk, doing chores, or, better yet, curled up by the fire with a good book. There will be leftovers and, for my children, that's the best part. I make "Beefy Noodles" by thickening the broth with a roux—equal parts flour and butter cooked together—and then adding slivers of beef and some penne pasta. That's the great thing about pot roast—it's good the first day and better the next.

1 chuck or rump roast (3 to 4 pounds)

Kosher salt

Freshly ground black pepper

All-purpose flour for dusting

$1/4$ cup olive oil

1 heel from celery bunch, halved, plus 4 celery
    stalks, chopped

1 yellow onion, quartered

2 bay leaves

2 cans (49 ounces each) low-sodium beef broth

1 pound baby carrots, peeled

1 pound baby new potatoes, quartered

Preheat the oven to 375°F. Season the roast well with salt and pepper and then dust the roast on all sides with a light coating of flour.

In a 6- to 8-quart Dutch oven over medium-high heat, warm the olive oil and brown the roast on all sides, adjusting the heat as needed to ensure even browning. Remove the roast from the pot, pour off the excess fat, and then return the meat to the pot. Add the heel of celery, the onion, bay leaves, and beef broth. The meat will be submerged in broth.

Cover the pot, place it in the oven, and roast the meat until it is just becoming tender, about $3^1/2$ hours. Remove from the oven, discard the vegetables and bay leaves, and use the side of a spoon to skim the surface of any fat. Scatter the carrots, potatoes, and chopped celery around the roast. Cover, return the pot to the oven, and continue roasting until the vegetables and meat are tender when pierced with a fork, about 40 minutes longer.

Carefully transfer the roast to a carving board and tent with aluminum foil. Skim all of the fat from the surface of the broth and then season to taste with salt and pepper. Slice the roast, arrange in warmed, shallow individual bowls, and spoon some vegetables around the meat. Ladle some broth over the top and serve immediately.

SIDE DISHES & BREADS

Rustic Roasted Vegetables

↔ serves 4 to 6

Enjoy the rustic character of these vegetables, which are simple and nutritious enough for a family meal and special enough for entertaining. They are especially delicious with Bistro Roasted Chicken (page 121). To make the dinnertime preparation easier, cut and combine the vegetables early in the day and then roast them just before serving.

HERB GARLIC OIL

1/2 cup extra-virgin olive oil

1 tablespoon chopped fresh rosemary

1 tablespoon chopped fresh thyme

1 tablespoon chopped fresh oregano

3 cloves garlic, minced

1 tablespoon kosher salt, plus salt to taste

4 small carrots, peeled

8 baby new potatoes

Ice water

2 ears corn, shucked and cut into thirds, crosswise

2 small zucchini, ends trimmed and
    quartered crosswise on the diagonal

1 yellow bell pepper, seeded, deribbed, and
    quartered lengthwise

1 red bell pepper, seeded, deribbed and
    quartered lengthwise

8 asparagus, tough ends removed

Freshly ground black pepper

To make the Herb Garlic Oil, in a small jar with a tight-fitting lid, combine the olive oil, rosemary, thyme, oregano, and garlic. Shake until well blended and then set aside.

To make the vegetables, preheat the oven to 400°F. Bring a large pot of water to a boil over medium-high heat, add 1 tablespoon salt, and then add the carrots and potatoes. Cook until almost tender when pierced with a knife, about 12 minutes. Using tongs or a slotted spoon, transfer the vegetables to a large bowl of ice water to stop the cooking. When cool, drain on a baking sheet lined with a double thickness of paper towels to absorb moisture. Add the corn to the boiling water and cook for 2 minutes. Transfer the corn to the ice water. When cool, drain and place on the baking sheet.

In a shallow roasting pan, arrange the carrots, potatoes, and corn in an even layer along with the zucchini, bell peppers, and asparagus. Shake the jar of Herb Garlic Oil until well blended and then drizzle it evenly over the vegetables. Season the vegetables with salt and pepper.

Roast the vegetables until they are nicely browned and crisp-tender, 15 to 20 minutes. Arrange on a platter and serve hot.

Ratatouille

↔ serves 6

Ratatouille, a specialty of Provence in southern France, is so adaptable that it can accompany almost any main course in this book. This recipe also makes a wonderful topping for Parmesan Polenta (page 166). Herbes de Provence is a well-known blend of dried herbs that reflects the traditional flavors of the region. It is available dried at gourmet grocery stores, but you can mix up your own blend from fresh herbs when they are available.

HERBES DE PROVENCE

$1/2$ teaspoon fennel seeds

1 teaspoon fresh or dried lavender buds (optional)

1 teaspoon chopped fresh marjoram

1 teaspoon chopped fresh rosemary

1 teaspoon chopped fresh sage

1 teaspoon fresh thyme leaves

$1/2$ cup or more extra-virgin olive oil, or as needed

3 cloves garlic, thinly sliced

1 shallot, thinly sliced

1 cup diced red onion ($3/4$-inch dice)

1 cup diced red bell pepper ($3/4$-inch dice)

1 cup diced green bell pepper ($3/4$-inch dice)

1 cup diced yellow summer squash ($3/4$-inch dice)

1 cup diced zucchini ($3/4$-inch dice)

2 cups diced eggplant ($3/4$-inch dice)

$1/2$ cup tomato paste

1 tablespoon chopped fresh basil

Kosher salt

Freshly ground black pepper

To make the Herbes de Provence, finely crush the fennel seeds. In a bowl stir together the crushed fennel, lavender (if using), marjoram, rosemary, sage, and thyme. Cover with plastic wrap and set aside in the refrigerator.

In a large skillet over medium heat, warm $1/4$ cup of the olive oil and swirl to coat the bottom of the pan. Add the garlic and shallot and sauté, stirring frequently, until softened but not brown, about 1 minute. Using a slotted spoon, transfer the garlic and shallot to a plate. Add the onion and bell peppers and sauté until lightly browned and very soft, about 15 minutes. Using the slotted spoon, transfer the onion and bell peppers to a plate. Repeat with the yellow squash and zucchini, adding more oil if needed, and sautéing until lightly browned, 10 to 12 minutes. Transfer them to a plate. Using the slotted spoon, scoop any browned bits from the oil.

Raise the heat to high, add the remaining $1/4$ cup olive oil to the skillet, and swirl to coat the bottom of the pan. Add the eggplant and sauté, stirring frequently, until the eggplant is lightly browned, about 8 minutes. Return all the sautéed vegetables to the skillet and sauté until heated through. Reduce the heat to medium and stir in the tomato paste. Add the basil, season to taste with salt and pepper, and then add the herb blend. Stir gently until the herbs are well distributed, remove from the heat, and serve immediately.

Maple Roast Acorn Squash

↔ serves 4

In early fall, when I see bushels of acorn squash brimming over at the farmers' market, I immediately think of this recipe. Use medium-sized squashes and serve straight from the oven, or scoop out the flesh and mash it with a splash of heavy cream.

2 acorn squashes

Kosher salt

Freshly ground black pepper

Freshly grated nutmeg

4 tablespoons ($^1/_2$ stick) unsalted butter

1$^1/_2$ cups pure maple syrup

Preheat the oven to 400°F. Cut the squashes into quarters, lengthwise. Scoop out and discard the seeds and strings. Cut a thin slice off the stem and blossom ends so that the halves will sit level. Place the halves on a rimmed baking sheet and sprinkle each half with a little salt and pepper. Grate a generous amount of nutmeg into each half. Place 1 tablespoon of the butter in each cavity. Fill each cavity, almost to the top, with the maple syrup.

Roast the squashes until the flesh is very tender when pierced with a knife, about 1 hour. Serve immediately.

Roasted Asparagus Gratin

↔ serves 6

In spring, when the first asparagus arrives in the market, I look for the jumbo spears and cook them as often as I can. You can grill, roast, sauté, or simply steam asparagus, but when you want to showcase it in a finished dish, make this luscious gratin. Serve the gratin as part of a brunch buffet, as a side dish with roast lamb or chicken, or in individual gratin dishes as a vegetarian main course.

2 pounds jumbo asparagus, tough ends removed
    and lower half of each spear peeled

3 tablespoons extra-virgin olive oil

Kosher salt

Freshly ground black pepper

1 tablespoon fresh lemon juice

1 tablespoon unsalted butter

1 clove garlic, minced

1 tablespoon minced shallot

2 cups heavy (whipping) cream

3/4 cup (3 ounces) freshly grated Parmesan cheese,
    preferably Parmigiano-Reggiano

2 tablespoons coarsely shaved Parmesan cheese,
    preferably Parmigiano-Reggiano

2 tablespoons unseasoned dried bread crumbs

Position a rack in the upper third of the oven and preheat the oven to 450°F. In a shallow baking dish, toss the asparagus with the olive oil, a little salt and pepper, and the lemon juice until the spears are evenly coated.

Roast the asparagus until the spears are just beginning to brown yet are still crisp and tender, about 12 minutes. Remove from the oven and drain off the excess oil.

Meanwhile, in a 2-quart saucepan over medium heat, melt the butter. Add the garlic and shallot and sauté, stirring constantly, until the shallot is translucent, about 2 minutes. Add the cream and simmer, uncovered, until reduced by one third, about 6 minutes. Stir in the grated Parmesan cheese and season to taste with salt and pepper.

Arrange the asparagus in an ovenproof serving dish and spoon the Parmesan cream sauce over the spears, allowing the tips and bases to remain uncovered. Scatter the shaved Parmesan over the top and sprinkle with the bread crumbs. Bake until nicely browned, about 5 minutes. Serve immediately.

Sizzling Mushrooms

↔ serves 4 to 6

In fall, mushrooms make the perfect accompaniment to just about any meal. Although this recipe calls for specific mushrooms, experiment with other varieties in the market. When making this dish, the goal is to roast the mushrooms so they are crispy on the outside, velvety inside, aromatic from the fresh herbs, and about as salty as popcorn.

$1/2$ pound oyster mushrooms, stems trimmed

$1/2$ pound very small button mushrooms, stems trimmed

$3/4$ pound portobello mushrooms, stems and black gills removed and caps cut into $1/2$-inch-thick slices

$1/2$ pound cremini mushrooms, stems trimmed

$1/2$ pound shiitake mushrooms, stems trimmed and large caps halved

6 tablespoons Herb Garlic Oil (page 154)

1 teaspoon chopped fresh sage

Kosher salt

Freshly ground black pepper

Lemon wedges

Fresh thyme sprigs

Position a rack in the upper third of the oven and preheat to 450°F. Place a large well-seasoned cast-iron skillet on the rack and heat until hot while the oven preheats.

In a large bowl, combine all of the mushrooms. Drizzle with the Herb Garlic Oil and add the sage. Toss until the mushrooms are evenly coated and then season with salt and pepper.

Carefully arrange the mushrooms in an even layer in the hot skillet and return the skillet to the same rack. Roast for 3 minutes. Stir the mushrooms and roast until nicely browned, 2 to 3 minutes longer.

Remove from the oven and transfer to a warmed serving dish. Garnish with the lemon wedges and thyme sprigs. Serve immediately.

Italian-Style Roasted
Brussels Sprouts ↔ serves 6

Brussels sprouts are one of the more maligned members of the cabbage family. They are cute to look at raw and fresh, but completely unappetizing when dull green from overcooking or, worse yet, waterlogged from boiling. Here's a recipe to save the poor sprouts! Choose the smallest Brussels sprouts available, as they are sweeter and milder in flavor. Serve the sprouts hot from the oven or at room temperature.

1¼ pounds Brussels sprouts, trimmed and
　　halved lengthwise

½ cup (1 stick) unsalted butter

2 tablespoons extra-virgin olive oil

3 cloves garlic, finely minced

Kosher salt

Freshly ground black pepper

Preheat the oven to 350°F. Using a paring knife, score the core of each Brussels sprout half. Place the sprouts in a bowl. In a small saucepan over medium heat, melt the butter. Add the olive oil and garlic and stir to mix. Pour the butter mixture over the sprouts and toss until they are well coated. Season with salt and pepper. Arrange in an even layer on a rimmed baking sheet.

Roast the Brussels sprouts until a knife easily pierces the center, 35 to 40 minutes. Transfer to a bowl and serve immediately or at room temperature.

Roasted Garlic Mashed Potatoes

↔ serves 6

I believe that no other side dish can win over friends as quickly as mashed potatoes. Here, I pack the potatoes with big flavor—lots of roasted garlic! I don't skimp on cream or butter, and the addition of sour cream is a final gesture of richness and simple pleasure. If serving a crowd, double this recipe. –CHEF DAVID SHAW

$2^1/_2$ pounds Idaho potatoes, peeled and cut into 2-inch chunks

2 large cloves fresh garlic

1 tablespoon kosher salt

2 tablespoons roasted garlic (page 14)

6 tablespoons ($^3/_4$ stick) unsalted butter

$^1/_2$ cup heavy (whipping) cream

$^1/_4$ teaspoon freshly ground white pepper

$^1/_4$ cup sour cream

In a large saucepan, combine the potatoes, fresh garlic, $1^1/_2$ teaspoons of the salt, and water to cover generously. Partially cover the pan and bring to a boil over high heat. Reduce the heat so the water boils gently and cook until the potatoes are very tender when pierced with a fork, 10 to 12 minutes.

Meanwhile, in a 2-quart saucepan, combine the roasted garlic, butter, cream, the remaining $1^1/_2$ teaspoons salt, white pepper, and sour cream. Bring to a simmer and then remove from the heat.

Drain the potatoes, return them to the warm pan, and place over low heat for 1 minute to evaporate any excess water. Use a potato masher, food mill, or a ricer to mash the potatoes, then slowly add the cream mixture and stir until the potatoes are as soft and moist as you like. Taste and adjust the seasoning. Serve immediately or keep warm in the top of a double boiler set over simmering water.

Gruyère and Custard Baked Potatoes ↔ serves 8

Gruyère cheese is named after the valley of the same name in Switzerland. This sweet, nutty cheese is formed into 100-pound wheels and aged for up to a year. Gruyère is the cheese that most often tops French onion soup. Make this gratin instead of mashed potatoes the next time you serve steaks, lamb, or prime rib. Do not worry if there are leftovers; they can be reheated easily (see Cook's Note).

1 tablespoon unsalted butter, at room temperature

4 large Idaho potatoes, peeled and sliced into
$1/4$ -inch-thick rounds

2 cups (8 ounces) shredded Gruyère cheese

8 large eggs

2 cups heavy (whipping) cream

1 teaspoon chicken bouillon granules

1 teaspoon kosher salt

$1/4$ teaspoon freshly ground white pepper

$1/8$ teaspoon freshly grated nutmeg

Preheat the oven to 350°F. Coat a large oval or 9-by-13-inch baking pan with the butter.

Arrange a layer of potato slices, slightly overlapping, in the bottom of the prepared dish. Top with a layer of the cheese. Repeat the layers twice, finishing with a light layer of cheese. In a bowl, whisk the eggs until well beaten. Add the cream, bouillon granules, salt, pepper, and nutmeg and whisk until well blended. Carefully pour the egg mixture over the layered potatoes and cheese. Cover with aluminum foil, sealing the edges well.

Bake the gratin until the center is soft and just beginning to set up, 45 to 60 minutes. Remove the foil and continue to bake until the center is firmly set and the potatoes are nicely browned, 20 to 30 minutes longer. Let rest for 5 minutes before serving.

Cook's Note: *The potatoes can be served immediately, or they can be cooled in the dish and reheated. To reheat the gratin, cut the potatoes into serving-sized squares or triangles, arrange 2 inches apart on a buttered, rimmed baking sheet, and then brush the tops with a little melted butter. Bake in a 400°F oven until heated through and nicely browned, 12 to 15 minutes. Serve immediately.*

Parmesan Polenta

↔ serves 6

Polenta is Italian–style cornmeal mush, and it is a fabulous alternative to potatoes. Top it with Parmesan, blend in cheese, serve it with Ratatouille (page 155), or spread it on a baking sheet, chill it, and then cut it into squares and grill or pan–fry it. In other words, polenta is versatile. –CHEF DAVID SHAW

6 cups water

2 teaspoons kosher salt, plus salt to taste

1$^{1}/_{2}$ cups coarse yellow cornmeal

3 tablespoons unsalted butter

$^{1}/_{2}$ cup (2 ounces) freshly grated Parmesan cheese,
　　preferably Parmigiano-Reggiano

Freshly ground black pepper

In a heavy, 4-quart saucepan over medium-high heat, bring the water to a boil. Reduce the heat to medium-low and add 2 teaspoons salt. Whisking constantly, add the cornmeal in a slow, steady stream. Adjust the heat so the polenta doesn't splatter and cook, stirring frequently, until all of the water is absorbed and the mixture is creamy, 18 to 20 minutes. Remove from the heat.

Stir in the butter and Parmesan and then season to taste with salt and pepper. Serve at once.

Mediterranean Couscous

↔ serves 4

There are two things, besides the flavor, that are wonderful about couscous: First, it's one of the easiest side dishes to make. And second, everyone is always surprised to learn that couscous is a pasta and not a grain. This couscous is flavor-packed with sun-dried tomatoes, olives, and herbs. –CHEF DAVID SHAW

$1/2$ cup dry-packed sun-dried tomatoes
(about $1^{1}/2$ ounces)

Boiling water

$2^{1}/4$ cups low-sodium chicken broth

3 tablespoons olive oil

$1^{1}/2$ cups quick-cooking couscous

$1/4$ cup dry-cured black olives, pitted and quartered

1 tablespoon Herbes de Provence (page 155)

1 tablespoon chopped fresh flat-leaf parsley

Kosher salt

Freshly ground black pepper

In a heatproof bowl, soak the sun-dried tomatoes in the boiling water to cover until softened, about 10 minutes. Drain and pat dry with paper towels. Coarsely chop and set aside.

Meanwhile, in a small saucepan over high heat, bring the chicken broth to a boil. In a 3-quart saucepan over medium-high heat, warm the oil and swirl to coat the bottom of the pan. Add the couscous and stir constantly until it is coated with the oil, about 1 minute. Add the broth all at once and bring to a boil. Reduce the heat to medium-low, cover, and simmer the couscous until all the liquid is absorbed, 8 to 10 minutes.

Remove from the heat and use a fork to fluff the couscous, breaking up any lumps. Add the chopped tomatoes, olives, Herbes de Provence, and parsley and stir gently. Taste and adjust seasoning with salt and pepper. Serve immediately.

Cast-Iron Skillet Corn Bread

↔ serves 6 to 8

I learned how to make this classic corn bread from my wife. Her family were all born and raised in northwest Tennessee. I was raised in Chicago and, as far as I knew, corn bread came as a mix in a box. I know better now! This skillet corn bread is a staple in our house. For the best results use a well-seasoned cast-iron skillet. –VINCENT ROSSETTI

$1/4$ cup vegetable oil

1 cup yellow cornmeal

$1/3$ cup all-purpose flour

1 teaspoon baking powder

$1/2$ teaspoon kosher salt

Freshly ground black pepper

1 large egg, beaten

1 cup buttermilk

2 tablespoons water

$1/2$ cup finely diced yellow onion (optional)

$1/2$ cup diced cooked bacon (optional)

$3/4$ cup canned whole kernel corn (optional)

Preheat the oven to 400°F. Pour the vegetable oil into a 10-inch cast-iron skillet and put the skillet in the oven while it preheats.

Meanwhile, in a large bowl, stir together the cornmeal, flour, baking powder, salt, and a few grindings of pepper.

In a bowl, whisk together the egg, buttermilk, and water until blended. Stir the liquid mixture into the dry ingredients, mixing together just until moist; a few lumps should be evident. Stir in any one or all of the optional ingredients, if desired.

Carefully pour the batter into the preheated oil in the pan. Bake the corn bread until the top is golden brown and the sides have pulled away from the pan, about 20 minutes. Serve immediately.

Focaccia
with Olive Oil and Rosemary ↪ serves 6 to 8

Once, on business in Verona, Italy, I happened upon a street scene just before dinnertime that caught my attention. A little bakery run by six Italian bakers had a long line of people waiting outside. I wondered what all of the fuss was about. Did this bakery have a variety of breads and pastries that enticed folks to stop? Once I got in the door and was immersed in aromas, sights, and sounds I realized the bakers offered one product and one product only—focaccia.

2 packages ($4^1/2$ teaspoons) active dry yeast

2 cups warm water (105° to 115°F)

1 tablespoon sugar

$5^1/3$ cups unbleached all-purpose flour

$2^1/2$ teaspoons kosher salt

$1/2$ cup extra-virgin olive oil

1 teaspoon chopped fresh rosemary

Freshly ground black pepper

In a bowl, using a wooden spoon, stir together the yeast, water, sugar, and 2 tablespoons of the flour. Let stand until foamy, about 10 minutes.

In a large bowl, stir together 5 cups of the flour and $1^1/2$ teaspoons of the salt, then form a well in the center. Pour the yeast mixture into the well along with 2 tablespoons of the olive oil. Stir with a wooden spoon, incorporating the ingredients until a soft dough forms. Use floured hands to mix the dough when it becomes too stiff to work with a spoon.

Dust a work surface with half of the remaining flour (about $1^1/2$ table-spoons). Turn the dough out onto the work surface and knead 10 min-utes, adding the flour if the dough becomes sticky. When the dough is smooth and elastic, shape it into a ball and place it back into the bowl with 1 tablespoon of the olive oil. Turn the dough once to coat. Cover the bowl with a damp cloth and allow the dough to rise in a warm place until doubled in bulk, 30 to 45 minutes. Punch down the dough, cover, and allow to rise again until doubled in bulk, about 35 minutes longer.

Use 1 tablespoon of the oil to grease an 11-by-15-inch rimmed baking sheet. On a lightly floured work surface, spread and press the dough flat until it is about the same size as the baking sheet. Place in the pre-pared pan. Cover with plastic wrap and let rise until doubled, about 15 minutes. Poke firmly into the dough, making a pattern. While the dough is completing its final rise, position a rack in the middle to upper two thirds of the oven and preheat to 425°F.

Sprinkle the dough with the rosemary, the remaining 1 teaspoon salt, and pepper. Drizzle evenly with the remaining 4 tablespoons olive oil. Bake until golden brown, 18 to 22 minutes. Serve piping hot.

Braided Challah

↔ makes 2 challahs; serves 12

For me, no holiday is complete without this challah on the table. I can't remember a holiday dinner that didn't include my grandfather's famous challah. Pop would spend all morning shaping and baking his bread to perfection; the glorious aromas drifted through the house, making everyone's mouth water in anticipation. Although Pop passed away in 1996, my family has carried on his tradition of baking challah for every family gathering. This is his famous recipe.
–REBECCA NICKEL

2 packages (4^1/$_2$ teaspoons) active dry yeast

2^1/$_4$ cups warm water (105° to 115°F)

2 tablespoons, plus ^{1}/$_2$ cup sugar

9 cups all-purpose flour

3 large eggs

1^1/$_2$ teaspoons kosher salt

^{1}/$_2$ cup (1 stick), plus 1 tablespoon unsalted
     butter or margarine, at room temperature

To make the sponge, using a stand mixer, combine the yeast, warm water, and 1 tablespoon of the sugar in the large mixer bowl. Allow to stand until foamy, about 5 minutes. Starting on low speed, mix in 2 cups of the flour, and then increase the speed to high and mix the sponge for 5 minutes. Remove the bowl from the mixer stand and let rise uncovered, in a warm place until light and bubbly, about 30 minutes.

Return the bowl to the mixer stand. With the mixer on low speed, mix in 2 of the eggs, the salt, ^{1}/$_2$ cup of the butter, the ^{1}/$_2$ cup sugar, and 6 cups of the flour. Beat until smooth and then mix in enough of the remaining 1 cup flour as needed to form a soft dough.

Dust a work surface with some of the remaining flour. Turn the dough out onto the work surface and knead until smooth and satiny, 10 to 12 minutes. Use additional flour only if the dough is sticky. Shape the dough into a ball. Grease a large bowl with the 1 tablespoon butter, place the dough in the bowl, and turn the dough to grease it on all sides. Cover the bowl with plastic wrap and allow the dough to rise in a warm place until doubled in bulk, 1^1/$_2$ to 2 hours.

Punch down the dough and then turn it out onto a barely floured work surface. Using a rolling pin, roll the dough into a 12-by-16-inch rectangle. Divide it lengthwise into 3 equal pieces. Divide 2 of the pieces into 3 strips each. Using your palm, roll each strip back and forth on the work surface to form a sausage shape about 16 inches long and $1\frac{1}{2}$ inches in diameter. Using 3 strips of dough for each loaf, form 2 braided loaves, tucking the ends under. Cut the remaining piece of dough lengthwise into 6 strips. Roll the strips into sausage shapes each 10 inches long and 1 inch in diameter, and make 2 smaller braids. Place 1 smaller braid lengthwise on top of each larger braid. Place the loaves side by side, but well spaced, on a well-greased baking sheet and allow to rise in a warm place until doubled in bulk, 45 to 50 minutes.

Beat the remaining egg with the remaining 1 tablespoon sugar. Brush each loaf liberally with the egg wash. Place in a cold oven and turn the oven to 350°F. Bake until the loaves are nicely browned on the top and bottom, 40 to 50 minutes. Let cool on a wire rack before slicing.

Savory Scones

↝ makes 8 large scones

A scone is a Scottish quick bread that takes its name from the Stone of Destiny (or scone), the place where Scottish kings were once crowned. Scones can be savory or sweet and are as quick to prepare as a biscuit, as they require no rising time before baking. These cheese–laden scones are great with a hearty soup or stew. Experiment to vary the flavorings and cheeses to match your menu. —TONY COLABELLI

$1/2$ cup (2 ounces) freshly grated Parmesan cheese

$1/2$ cup (2 ounces) shredded Cheddar cheese

2 teaspoons chopped fresh rosemary

2 teaspoons chopped fresh thyme

2 teaspoons chopped fresh flat-leaf parsley

$2^1/2$ cups all-purpose flour

1 tablespoon baking powder

$1/2$ teaspoon kosher salt

$1/2$ cup (1 stick) ice-cold unsalted butter,
      cut into small cubes

2 large eggs, beaten

$1/2$ cup buttermilk

$1/2$ cup heavy (whipping) cream,
      plus more for brushing

Preheat the oven to 350°F. Line a baking sheet with parchment paper.

In a small bowl, stir together 1 tablespoon of the Parmesan cheese, 2 tablespoons of the Cheddar cheese, and $1/2$ teaspoon each of the rosemary, thyme, and parsley. Set aside for topping the scones.

In a large bowl, sift together the flour, baking powder, and salt. Scatter the butter over the top. Using a pastry blender, cut the butter into the flour mixture until it resembles coarse crumbs. Using a wooden spoon, and with a few quick strokes, mix in the eggs, buttermilk, and the $1/2$ cup cream. Again with a few quick strokes, mix in the remaining Parmesan and Cheddar cheeses, rosemary, thyme, and parsley.

Turn the dough out onto a lightly floured work surface and divide the dough in half. Pat each half out into an 8-inch circle. Cut each circle into quarters and arrange the quarters on the prepared baking sheet. Brush the top of each scone with a little cream, and then sprinkle each with some of the reserved cheese-herb topping.

Bake the scones until golden brown, rotating the pan 180 degrees at the halfway point to ensure even browning, 20 to 25 minutes. Serve immediately.

Angel Biscuits

↪ makes 10 to 12 biscuits

A biscuit hot from the oven is a joy to eat. This recipe creates featherlight biscuits that will complement most any meal— great with barbecue, a natural with soups and stews, traditional with a fried chicken dinner. The trick to making biscuits fluffy, light, and tender is to handle the dough as little as possible. –RENEE DUVALL-NORTHERN

2¹/₂ cups self-rising flour, plus more for dusting

1 teaspoon kosher salt

3 tablespoons sugar

³/₄ cup ice-cold solid vegetable shortening,
     cut into small pieces

1 cup milk

Preheat the oven to 400°F. Have ready an ungreased baking sheet.

In a large bowl, stir together the flour, salt, and sugar. Scatter the shortening over the top. Using a pastry blender, cut the shortening into the flour mixture until it is crumbly and coarsely grainy. Using a large wooden spoon, stir in the milk just until the mixture begins to form a mass. Transfer the dough to a floured work surface, gathering all the loose bits, and knead it a dozen times, but no more. If the dough is too sticky, add a little flour, but not too much; the dough should stick to your hands a little.

Using your hands, flatten the biscuit dough into a disk about ³/₄ inch thick. Using a 2-inch round biscuit cutter, cut out as many biscuits as you can. Gather up the dough scraps and gently form into a disk. Cut out more biscuits. Arrange the biscuits 1 inch apart on the baking sheet.

Bake the biscuits until they are lightly browned, 14 to 17 minutes. Serve immediately.

DESSERTS

Millie's Pound Cake

↔ serves 10 to 12

I will always treasure this delicious Southern recipe given to me by my dear friend Millie Schoop. It brings to mind many an hour of strong coffee, lively conversation, comfort, and laughter. This cake is wonderful when served with a combination of berries. Our favorite is a mixture of blueberries and raspberries. —ELLEN GOVEDARE

1 1/2 cups (3 sticks) unsalted butter, at room
   temperature, plus more for preparing pan

3 cups all-purpose flour, plus more for
   preparing pan

1 package (8 ounces) cream cheese,
   at room temperature

3 cups granulated sugar

1 tablespoon pure vanilla extract

1 teaspoon almond extract

6 large eggs, at room temperature

TOPPING

1/4 cup powdered sugar

Whipped cream

1 to 2 pints berries

Position a rack in the lower third of the oven and preheat to 325°F. Butter a 10-inch tube pan and then dust the pan with flour, tapping out the excess.

In a large bowl, using an electric mixer set on high speed, beat together the 1 1/2 cups butter, cream cheese, and granulated sugar until light and fluffy. Add the vanilla and almond extracts and beat until incorporated. Add the eggs one at a time, beating well after each addition. Stop the mixer, scrape down the sides using a rubber spatula, and then beat on high speed for 1 minute longer. Reduce the speed to low and add the flour 1 cup at a time, beating after each addition just until the flour disappears. Do not overmix. Spoon the batter into the prepared pan and spread it evenly with a rubber spatula.

Bake the cake until a toothpick inserted into the top comes out clean, about 1 1/4 hours. Remove from the oven and let the cake rest in the pan on a wire rack for 15 minutes. Invert a rack on top of the cake, invert the cake and rack, and then lift off the pan. Let cool slightly.

Using a fine-mesh sieve, dust the top with powdered sugar while still warm. Cut into thick slices and serve warm with a dollop of whipped cream and fresh berries.

Mocha Java Cake

↦ serves 10

Nordstrom has always been passionate about coffee and, in fact, opened one of Seattle's first espresso bars back in 1980, when Starbucks had just one location. Since that time, the offering of freshly brewed coffee has become a traditional greeting at each Nordstrom location. In tribute to this tradition, I am contributing this coffee–infused cake, a longtime specialty of my mother. It is great topped with some decadent coffee ice cream. —JOSEPH BOUNDS

$1^1/_2$ cups (3 sticks) unsalted butter, plus more
    for preparing pan

3 cups all-purpose flour, plus more
    for preparing pan

3 bars (4 ounces each) bittersweet chocolate,
    finely chopped

$1^1/_4$ teaspoons baking soda

$1/_4$ teaspoon kosher salt

$2^1/_4$ cups sugar

3 large eggs

2 cups espresso or very strong coffee, cooled

$1^1/_2$ teaspoons pure vanilla extract

1 teaspoon almond extract

Preheat the oven to 325°F. Butter a 10-inch tube pan and then dust the pan with flour, tapping out the excess.

Bring 1 inch of water to a simmer in the bottom of a double boiler or saucepan. Place the chocolate and $1^1/_2$ cups butter in the top of the double boiler or in a heatproof bowl placed over the pan, and heat, stirring frequently, until melted and smooth. Transfer to a large bowl. Set aside to cool for 5 minutes.

In a bowl, stir together the 3 cups flour, baking soda, and salt. Gradually beat the sugar into the melted chocolate-butter mixture until well combined. Add the eggs one at a time, beating well after each addition. Continue beating while slowly adding the espresso and the vanilla and almond extracts. Add the dry ingredients and mix just until all the flour disappears. Pour and scrape the batter into the prepared pan; it will come almost to the top. Smooth the top, making sure the batter is evenly distributed in the pan.

Bake the cake until a toothpick inserted into the center comes out clean, 60 to 65 minutes. Remove from the oven and let the cake rest in the pan on a wire rack for 10 minutes before inverting onto a cake plate. Let cool to room temperature before serving.

Classic Carrot Cake

↔ serves 12

Carrot cake has long been offered at Café Nordstrom. There is something special about watching a group of friends gathered around a table talking, smiling, and happily eating moist slices of carrot cake and drinking hot cups of coffee. This recipe is dense, sweet, and refreshingly moist. —FARIS ZOMA

Unsalted butter for preparing pan

1$\frac{1}{2}$ cups all-purpose flour, plus more for

    preparing pan

1$\frac{1}{4}$ cups granulated sugar

1 cup plus 2 tablespoons canola oil

3 large eggs

1$\frac{1}{2}$ teaspoons pure vanilla extract

$\frac{1}{2}$ teaspoon kosher salt

1$\frac{1}{2}$ teaspoons baking soda

2 $\frac{1}{4}$ cups finely grated, peeled carrots

1 cup chopped walnuts, toasted

    (see Cook's Note, page 190)

2 teaspoons ground cinnamon

CREAM CHEESE FROSTING

$\frac{3}{4}$ pound cream cheese, at room temperature

$\frac{1}{2}$ cup (1 stick) unsalted butter,

    at room temperature

1 cup powdered sugar

1$\frac{1}{2}$ teaspoons pure vanilla extract

2 cups chopped walnuts, toasted

    (see Cook's Note, page 190)

Preheat the oven to 350°F. Lightly butter two 9-inch round cake pans and then dust the pans with flour, tapping out the excess.

In a bowl, using an electric mixer set on low speed, beat together the sugar and canola oil until blended. Add the eggs one at a time, beating well after each addition. Add the vanilla and salt, then slowly add the 1$\frac{1}{2}$ cups flour and baking soda and beat just until smooth.

In a bowl, stir together the carrots, walnuts, and cinnamon, folding them into the batter until well distributed. Divide the batter evenly between the prepared pans, smoothing the top with the spatula.

Bake the cake layers until a toothpick inserted near the center of each cake comes out clean, 40 to 50 minutes. Remove from the oven and let the cakes rest in the pans on wire racks for 10 minutes. Place a rack on top of 1 cake, invert the cake and rack, and then lift off the pan. Repeat with the second cake. Let cool completely before icing.

To make the Cream Cheese Frosting, in a bowl, using the electric mixer set on medium speed, beat together the cream cheese, butter, powdered sugar, and vanilla until smooth. Increase the mixer speed to high and beat until the frosting increases in volume by about a half.

To assemble the cake, place 1 cake layer on a plate, bottom-side up. Cut strips of waxed paper and place under the edges of the cake to keep the plate clean while frosting the cake. Spread the top of this layer with about one third of the frosting. Place the second layer, bottom-side up, on top. Spread frosting around the sides of the cake, and then frost the top. Press a layer of chopped walnuts all around the sides. Carefully remove the strips of waxed paper. Cover and refrigerate the cake until serving.

Chocolate Paradise Cake

↔ serves 12

This is a traditional devil's food cake with bittersweet chocolate frosting. What makes this cake special and doubly decadent is the English toffee sprinkled over the frosting in the center of the cake and then pressed into the frosting all around the outside of the cake. A dusting of cocoa powder tops the cake. The final extravagance comes when the cake is served. Each slice is arranged on a plate in a pool of rich, luscious caramel sauce.

DEVIL'S FOOD CAKE

$^3/_4$ cup (1$^1/_2$ sticks) unsalted butter, at room
    temperature, plus more for preparing pan

2$^1/_4$ cups all-purpose flour, plus more for
    preparing pan

1 cup unsweetened cocoa powder, sifted

1$^1/_2$ teaspoons baking powder

$^1/_2$ teaspoon baking soda

$^1/_2$ teaspoon kosher salt

2 cups firmly packed light brown sugar

2 teaspoons pure vanilla extract

4 large eggs

1$^1/_2$ cups sour cream

Preheat the oven to 350°F. Lightly butter the bottoms and sides of two 9-inch round cake pans. Line the bottom of the pans with parchment and then butter the parchment. Dust the pans with flour, coating the bottoms and sides, and then tap out the excess.

In a large bowl, sift together the 2$^1/_4$ cups flour, cocoa powder, baking powder, baking soda, and salt. In another large bowl, using an electric mixer set on medium speed, beat the $^3/_4$ cup butter until creamy. Add the brown sugar and continue beating for 1 minute. Add the vanilla and continue beating until incorporated. Add the eggs one at a time, beating well after each addition. The butter mixture will look separated and grainy, which is not a problem. Beat in the sour cream and then add the flour mixture in 3 batches. The batter will be quite thick. Divide the batter evenly between the prepared pans, using a rubber spatula to spread the batter evenly.

Bake the cake layers until a toothpick inserted near the center of each cake comes out clean, about 30 minutes. Remove from the oven and let the cakes rest in the pans on wire racks for 10 minutes. Place a rack on top of 1 cake, invert the cake and rack, and then lift off the pan. Peel off the parchment circle. Repeat with the second cake. Let cool completely.

continued

BITTERSWEET CHOCOLATE FROSTING

12 ounces bittersweet chocolate, chopped

1 3/4 cups heavy (whipping) cream

1/2 cup sour cream

Pinch of kosher salt

GARNISH

2 cups coarsely crushed English toffee

2 to 3 tablespoons unsweetened cocoa powder

SERVING

2 cups homemade or store-bought caramel sauce, warmed

To make the Bittersweet Chocolate Frosting, bring 1 inch of water to a simmer in the bottom of a double boiler or saucepan. Place the chocolate and cream in the top of the double boiler or in a heatproof bowl placed over the pan, and heat, stirring occasionally, until the chocolate melts and the chocolate and cream are mixed together and smooth. Remove from the heat and stir in the sour cream and salt. Set aside to cool. When cool, using an electric mixer set on medium speed, beat the frosting until it is thick enough to spread and nearly double in volume.

To assemble and decorate the cake, using a pastry brush, brush off any loose crumbs from the sides and tops of the cake layers. Using a serrated knife, trim the domed tops of the cake layers, making them level. Place 1 layer on a cake plate, bottom-side up. Cut strips of waxed paper and place under the edges of the cake to keep the cake plate clean while frosting the cake. Spread the top of this layer with about one fourth of the frosting. Top the frosting with 1/2 cup of the crushed toffee. Place the second layer, bottom-side up, on top and gently press it into place. Spread frosting all around the sides of the cake and then frost the top of the cake. Using the remaining toffee, press it all around the sides of the cake. Using a fine-mesh sieve, sift a healthy dusting of cocoa powder over the top of the cake. Carefully remove the strips of waxed paper.

When ready to serve, slice the cake and serve each slice centered in a pool of warm caramel sauce.

"Easy as Pie" Crust

↦ makes enough dough for five 9-inch crusts

I have always prided myself on my pies, but I know that saying "easy as pie" can be misleading. I got this recipe from a friend's mother, and pie making has been an absolute joy for me ever since. No longer am I frantically patching the split edges of dough with water as I try to form a perfect circle. With this pie dough, I just press the dough back together and keep rolling. I've also found that juicy berry pies don't get as soggy with this crust. An added bonus: This recipe yields five single crusts, so you can portion and freeze the dough for future pies. —COLLENE LYNCH

4 cups all-purpose flour

1 tablespoon sugar

2 teaspoons kosher salt

1³/₄ cups ice-cold solid vegetable shortening,
    cut into small cubes

¹/₂ cup ice-cold water

1 large egg

1 tablespoon fresh lemon juice or cider vinegar

In a large bowl, stir together the flour, sugar, and salt. Using a pastry blender or 2 knives, cut the shortening into the flour mixture until it resembles coarse meal. In a small bowl using a fork, mix together the water, egg, and lemon juice until blended. Add the water mixture to the flour mixture and mix with a fork just until it comes together and forms a mass.

Transfer the dough to a floured work surface, gathering all the loose bits, and divide into 5 equal balls. Flatten to form disks, wrap each individually in plastic wrap, and refrigerate for at least 15 minutes before rolling out. Double wrap, label, and freeze any dough you won't be using within 3 days; thaw in the refrigerator. The dough can be frozen for up to 1 month.

Evelyn's Chocolate Cheesecake

↔ serves 10 to 12

Cheesecake, one of my family's favorite desserts, inspired me to develop this recipe, which has since gained some notoriety among my friends and family. Evelyn, my sister-in-law, asked for the recipe and I gladly shared it with her. One night, my wife and I had friends over for dinner. I proudly brought out my prized cheesecake, smugly expecting the customary oohs and aahs. Our guests took one look and said, "It looks wonderful Jonathon, but you really should try Evelyn's cheesecake. It's the best!" We now refer to this recipe as "Evelyn's Cheesecake." –JONATHON ASHMORE

GRAHAM CRACKER CRUST

4 tablespoons (1/2 stick) unsalted butter, melted

3/4 cup graham cracker crumbs (about 10 crackers)

1/4 cup old-fashioned rolled oats

3 tablespoons sugar

CREAM CHEESE FILLING

**3 packages (8 ounces each) cream cheese,
    at room temperature**

3/4 cup sugar

1/2 cup sour cream

3 large whole eggs, plus 1 large egg yolk

1 teaspoon pure vanilla extract

GANACHE TOPPING

3/4 cup heavy (whipping) cream

1 teaspoon unsalted butter

12 ounces semisweet chocolate, finely chopped

To make the Graham Cracker Crust, preheat the oven to 350°F. Butter a 10-inch springform pan with 1 tablespoon of the melted butter.

In a bowl, stir together the graham cracker crumbs, oats, and sugar. Stir in the remaining 3 tablespoons of butter until the mixture is evenly moistened. Press the crumb mixture firmly onto the bottom and halfway up the sides of the prepared pan. Bake until the crust is crisp and set, 5 to 6 minutes. Transfer to a wire rack. Leave the oven set at 350°F.

To make the Cream Cheese Filling, in a food processor fitted with the metal blade, process the cream cheese until light and fluffy. Add the sugar, sour cream, whole eggs, egg yolk, and the vanilla and process until smooth and thoroughly combined. (If using an electric mixer, add and mix the ingredients in the same order, using medium speed and stopping once to scrape down the sides of the bowl.) Carefully pour the batter into the prebaked crust.

Bake the cheesecake for 10 minutes. Reduce the oven temperature to 325°F and continue baking until the edges of the cake are puffed and somewhat separated from the pan, yet the center appears to be soft but not too wet, about 35 minutes longer. At this point, turn the oven off and leave the door slightly ajar with the cheesecake inside to continue setting up for about 35 minutes. Transfer to a wire rack and let cool completely in the pan.

To make the Ganache Topping, in a small saucepan over low heat, bring the cream and butter to a simmer. Stir in the chocolate and immediately remove from the heat. Cover and let stand for 5 minutes. Remove the cover and gently stir until all of the chocolate is melted and the ganache is smooth. Let cool for 10 minutes.

Remove the sides from the springform pan and transfer the cake to a serving plate. Spread the ganache evenly over the top of the cheesecake. Cover and refrigerate for at least 4 hours before serving.

To cut dip the knife blade in hot water before cutting each slice, and wipe the knife clean after each cut.

Pumpkin Frangelico Cheesecake

↔ serves 10 to 12

Deciding on a menu for Thanksgiving dinner challenges the cook who wants to blend tradition with exploration. This cheesecake plays on the classic pumpkin-for-dessert theme, but twists the tradition away from pie. Unlike a pumpkin pie, which tastes best the day it is baked, this pumpkin cheesecake can be made several days ahead and refrigerated. This is a boon to the busy Thanksgiving cook.

For those not familiar with Frangelico liqueur, it is a hazelnut-flavored liqueur, enhanced by a secret formula of flower and berry essences. Its flavor is a delightful complement to the pumpkin and all the sweet spices in this cheesecake.

HAZELNUT GRAHAM CRACKER CRUST

$^1/_2$ cup (1 stick) unsalted butter, melted

2 cups graham cracker crumbs (about 25 crackers)

$^1/_2$ cup chopped hazelnuts, toasted
    (see Cook's Note, page 190)

PUMPKIN FRANGELICO FILLING

3 packages (8 ounces each) cream cheese,
    at room temperature

5 large eggs, lightly beaten

1$^1/_2$ cups firmly packed dark brown sugar

$^1/_2$ cup Frangelico liqueur

1 teaspoon pure vanilla extract

1 teaspoon ground cinnamon

$^1/_2$ teaspoon ground ginger

$^1/_4$ teaspoon freshly grated nutmeg

$^1/_8$ teaspoon ground cloves

1 can (15 ounces) unsweetened pumpkin purée

To make the Hazelnut Graham Cracker Crust, preheat the oven to 375°F. Butter a 10-inch springform pan with 1 tablespoon of the melted butter.

In a bowl, stir together the graham cracker crumbs and hazelnuts. Stir in the remaining 7 tablespoons of butter until the mixture is evenly moistened. Press the crumbs firmly onto the bottom and halfway up the sides of the pan. Bake until the crust is crisp and set, about 8 minutes. Transfer to a wire rack. Reduce the oven temperature to 350°F.

To make the Pumpkin Frangelico Filling, in a food processor fitted with the metal blade, process the cream cheese until light and fluffy. Add the eggs, brown sugar, Frangelico, vanilla, cinnamon, ginger, nutmeg, and cloves and process until smooth and thoroughly combined. Add the pumpkin purée and process until the mixture is light, about 1 minute. (If using an electric mixer, add and mix the ingredients in the same order, using high speed and stopping once to scrape down the sides of the bowl.) Carefully pour the batter into the prebaked crust.

Bake the cheesecake until the edges are puffed and somewhat separated from the pan, yet the center appears to be soft but not too wet, 60 to 70 minutes. At this point, turn the oven off and leave the door slightly ajar with the cheesecake inside to continue setting up for about 1 hour. Transfer to a wire rack and let cool completely in the pan. Cover and refrigerate until cold, several hours or overnight.

continued

FRANGELICO SOUR CREAM TOPPING

2 cups sour cream

$1/4$ cup granulated sugar

$1/4$ cup Frangelico liqueur

To make the Frangelico Sour Cream Topping, preheat the oven to 400°F. In a small bowl, stir together the sour cream, granulated sugar, and Frangelico until well blended and smooth. Pour the topping over the top of the cheesecake and use a rubber spatula to smooth the surface. Bake for 10 minutes to set the topping.

To serve, remove the sides from the springform pan and transfer the cake to a serving plate. To cut, dip the knife in hot water before cutting each slice, and wipe the knife clean after each cut.

COOK'S NOTE: *To toast sesame seeds, pine nuts, or slivered almonds, heat the seeds or nuts in a small, dry nonstick skillet over medium heat, stirring occasionally, until they start to sizzle and brown. Remove from the heat, transfer to a plate, and let cool. For other nuts such as pecans, walnuts, and hazelnuts, spread them on a rimmed baking sheet and toast in a 375°F oven until lightly browned, 8 to 12 minutes, depending on the type and size of the nut.*

1927 Cream Pie

↔ serves 8

My great-grandmother won a gold-medal brooch for sending this recipe to a competition sponsored by a Denver farm newspaper in 1927. It was undoubtedly made with nothing but fresh farm ingredients. Today, my family enjoys this incredibly simple creation with a dollop of whipped cream and a few strawberries and blueberries for garnish.
—JESSICA BLACK

9-inch unbaked pie crust

   (see Cook's Note)

3 large egg whites, at room temperature

$^3/_4$ cup sugar

1 rounded tablespoon all-purpose flour

Pinch of salt

1$^3/_4$ cups heavy (whipping) cream

$^1/_2$ teaspoon pure vanilla extract

OPTIONAL GARNISH

1 cup heavy (whipping) cream, whipped

1 pint strawberries

1 pint blueberries

Preheat the oven to 375°F. Have ready the unbaked pie crust.

Using an electric mixer set on medium speed, beat the egg whites until foamy. Increase the speed to high and beat until stiff. Continue beating, adding the sugar a little at a time until all the sugar is incorporated. Beat in the flour and salt. Slowly add the cream and vanilla and beat until well mixed. Pour into the unbaked pie crust.

Bake the pie until the top is beautifully browned and the filling is softly set and has risen like a soufflé, 45 to 55 minutes. Transfer the pie to a wire rack and let cool completely. Though the filling rises while baking, it will settle when removed from the oven. Garnish each serving with whipped cream and berries, if desired.

COOK'S NOTE: *This pie is too good to pass up! If you are in a hurry or panic at the thought of making your own pie crust, buy a frozen unbaked pie crust. You can also use your own favorite recipe or the recipe for "Easy as Pie" Crust on page 185. The latter makes a terrific crust, and you'll have extra dough to put in the freezer, ready for your next pie. For this pie, all you need to do is roll out the dough on a lightly floured surface into an 11-inch round, drape the dough over the rolling pin, and carefully transfer it to a 9-inch pie pan. Ease the dough into the bottom and sides of the pan, press it gently in place, and then trim the overhang to 1 inch. Fold the overhang under itself and flute the edge attractively.*

White Chocolate Bread Pudding

↔ serves 12

This is our most popular dessert at Cafe Bistro. No matter how well you have dined, or how much you have eaten, there is always room for this special treat. It is a perfect dessert for entertaining because most of the work can be done in advance. The pudding is baked twice; before it goes into the oven the second time, it is brushed with butter so it develops a crisp, yet delicate, exterior and a smooth, velvety, and seductive interior. We always serve this dessert with White Chocolate Sauce, Raspberry Sauce, fresh raspberries, and delicate ribbons of shaved white chocolate. Yummm.

5 tablespoons ($^1/_2$ stick) unsalted butter, melted

4 cups heavy (whipping) cream

2 cups milk

1 cup sugar

3$^1/_2$ cups (about 1$^1/_3$ pounds) white
    chocolate morsels

6 large whole eggs, plus 12 large egg yolks

1 teaspoon pure vanilla extract

1 24-inch loaf day-old French bread,
    cut into $^1/_2$-inch-thick slices

Preheat the oven to 325°F. Brush a 9-by-13-by-2-inch baking pan with 2 tablespoons melted butter. Line the bottom of the pan with parchment paper.

In a 4-quart saucepan over medium heat, combine the cream, milk, and sugar and heat just until hot. Remove from the heat, add the chocolate morsels, and stir until melted. Set aside to cool slightly.

In a large bowl, whisk together the whole eggs, egg yolks, and vanilla. Whisking constantly, gradually drizzle the warm cream mixture into the eggs, continuing to whisk until smooth and well blended. (If the cream mixture is too hot, the eggs will curdle.)

Lay half of the bread slices in the bottom of the prepared pan. Pour half of the cream mixture over the bread and allow to absorb the liquid, about 5 minutes. Layer the remaining bread on top and pour the rest of the cream mixture over it. Press down on the bread, making certain it completely absorbs the liquid. Cover the pan with aluminum foil.

Bake the pudding for 1 hour. Uncover and continue to bake until the liquid in the center has evaporated and the pudding is golden brown, about 30 minutes longer. Transfer to a wire rack and let cool completely.

continued

RASPBERRY SAUCE

1/2 cup water

1/2 cup sugar

2 teaspoons grated orange zest

2 cups fresh or unsweetened frozen raspberries

WHITE CHOCOLATE SAUCE

1/2 cup heavy (whipping) cream

1 cup white chocolate morsels

GARNISH

1 pint fresh raspberries

4-ounce chunk white chocolate

When the bread pudding is cool, cover and refrigerate until cold. Run a sharp knife between the edges of the bread pudding and the sides of the pan to loosen the pudding and then invert the pan onto a cutting board and tap the bottom to release the pudding. Peel off the parchment paper. Trim off the crusty edges around the sides. Cut the bread pudding into six 2-by-3-inch rectangles and then cut each rectangle in half on an angle to form 2 triangles. Wrap and store in the refrigerator.

To make the Raspberry Sauce, in a small saucepan over medium-high heat, combine the water, sugar, and orange zest and cook, stirring frequently, until the mixture is thick and syrupy, about 3 minutes. Add the raspberries, reduce the heat to low, and cook until the fruit begins to fall apart, about 3 minutes. Remove from the heat and let cool slightly. Then, using the back of a spoon, force the sauce through a fine-mesh sieve placed over a bowl to remove the seeds. Set aside until ready to serve.

To make the White Chocolate Sauce, in a small saucepan over medium-high heat, warm the cream until hot. Remove from the heat, add the chocolate morsels, and stir constantly until the chocolate is completely melted and the sauce is smooth. Keep warm.

To finish and assemble the dessert, preheat the oven to 350ºF. Butter a rimmed baking sheet and place the bread pudding triangles on it, leaving space between the pieces. Brush the triangles with the remaining melted butter. Bake the triangles until heated through and lightly browned, about 12 minutes.

For each serving, stand a hot bread pudding triangle on its side in the center of a large dessert plate. Run a stripe of White Chocolate Sauce across the plate, including over the top of the pudding. Pool some of the Raspberry Sauce at opposite edges of the plate. Garnish with raspberries and with ribbons of white chocolate cut from the chunk with a vegetable peeler.

White Chocolate Mousse

↔ serves 6

This simple recipe is a great way to dress up fresh berries in the summertime. It's also terrific served with Renee's Lemon Bars (page 206), or as a decadent complement to Crème Brûlée (page 198) with fresh berries. For an elegant presentation, pipe the mousse into stemmed glasses, using a pastry bag with a star-tip nozzle, and garnish with berries or shaved bittersweet chocolate.

8 ounces premium white chocolate, cut into chunks

2 cups heavy (whipping) cream

$1/4$ teaspoon pure vanilla extract

Pinch of kosher salt

Bring 1 inch of water to a simmer in the bottom of a double boiler or saucepan. Place the chocolate, cream, vanilla, and salt in the top of the double boiler or in a heatproof bowl placed over the pan, and heat, stirring occasionally, until the chocolate melts and the chocolate and cream are mixed together and smooth. Remove from the heat and place in the refrigerator for 20 to 30 minutes to cool completely.

Using an electric mixer set on high speed, beat the cooled chocolate mixture until it is light and fluffy, like a dense whipped cream. Refrigerate for 1 hour before serving.

Granny Smith Apple Crisp

↔ serves 6

Apple crisp is a perfect down–home dessert that is quicker to prepare than a traditional apple pie. Many types of apples will work with this recipe; it all depends on what texture and taste you want. Sauce apples, such as Cortland and McIntosh, collapse readily, creating a soft filling. Baking apples, such as Golden Delicious and Rome Beauty, hold their shape and texture for a longer time in the oven. Granny Smith apples fall somewhere in between, so everybody's happy! —RENEE DUVALL-NORTHERN

TOPPING

$1/2$ cup firmly packed light brown sugar

$1/3$ cup granulated sugar

1 teaspoon ground cinnamon

Pinch of freshly grated nutmeg

7 tablespoons all-purpose flour

Pinch of kosher salt

$1/2$ cup (1 stick) ice-cold unsalted butter, cut into small cubes

1 cup old-fashioned rolled oats

5 large Granny Smith apples, peeled, cored, and cut into wedges (about 6 cups)

$1/2$ teaspoon ground cinnamon

$1/3$ cup hot water

Preheat the oven to 350°F. Lightly butter an 8-inch square or 9-inch round baking pan.

To make the topping, in a bowl, stir together the brown sugar, granulated sugar, cinnamon, nutmeg, flour, and salt. Add the butter and oats. Using your fingers, a pastry blender, or a fork, work in the butter until all the ingredients are well blended but not overmixed. Refrigerate until ready to use.

To assemble the crisp, spread the apples in an even layer in the prepared pan and sprinkle with the cinnamon. Drizzle the water evenly over the apples. Spread the topping over the fruit.

Bake the crisp until the topping is brown and crunchy and the apples are tender, 25 to 30 minutes. Serve the crisp hot, warm, or at room temperature.

Crème Brûlée

↔ serves 6

Crème brûlée, *French for "burnt cream," is custard with a thin, brittle caramelized sugar topping. Although the topping can be created in a broiler, it is quicker and more effective to use a small propane torch.*

6 large egg yolks

3/4 cup sugar, plus more for sprinkling

3 cups heavy (whipping) cream

1 vanilla bean, halved lengthwise

1/2 pint raspberries

3 tablespoons shaved white chocolate

Preheat the oven to 300°F. Have ready six 3/4-cup ovenproof custard cups or ramekins set in a baking pan large enough to hold them without crowding.

In a large bowl, whisk together the egg yolks and 3/4 cup sugar until pale yellow and fairly thick.

In a 2-quart saucepan over medium heat, combine the cream and vanilla bean and heat just until steam rises. Cover the pan, remove from the heat, and let steep for 10 minutes. Remove the vanilla bean, and with the flat side of a paring knife, scrape out the seeds. Return the seeds to the cream and discard the pod. Whisking constantly, gradually drizzle the cream into the egg yolk mixture, continuing to whisk until smooth and well blended. (If the cream is too hot, the eggs will curdle.)

Divide the cream mixture evenly among the custard cups. Pour hot water into the baking pan to reach halfway up the sides of the molds. Bake the custards until they are just set—a little wobbly in the middle but definitely not runny when the baking pan is nudged—25 to 30 minutes. If your oven heats unevenly, you may need to rotate the pan 180 degrees at the halfway point. Remove the ramekins from the water bath, let cool on wire racks, and then cover and refrigerate until the custards are chilled.

About 10 minutes before serving, adjust the oven rack so it is 5 to 6 inches from the heat source and preheat the broiler. Sprinkle about 1 teaspoon of sugar evenly over the top of each custard. Place the custards under the broiler and, watching carefully, broil until the sugar is caramelized and a thin, glasslike coating forms on top, 1 to 2 minutes. Serve at once, garnished with the raspberries and white chocolate.

Triple-Chocolate Cookies

↳ makes 3 to 4 dozen cookies

Cookies are among the most popular desserts at Café Nordstrom. Few combinations are more satisfying than the taste of a cookie hot from the oven served with a glass of cold milk. These decadent, sweet bites are packed with chocolate three ways—cocoa powder, bars, and morsels. —CHEF TONY COLABELLI

1 cup (2 sticks) unsalted butter, at room
    temperature, plus more for preparing
    baking sheets

2 cups all-purpose flour

$^2/_3$ cup unsweetened cocoa powder

1 teaspoon baking soda

1 teaspoon kosher salt

1 pound bittersweet chocolate, cut into chunks

2 cups firmly packed light brown sugar

4 large eggs

1$^1/_3$ cups (8 ounces) white chocolate morsels

1 cup walnut halves, toasted
    (see Cook's Note, page 190)

Preheat the oven to 350°F. Lightly butter 2 baking sheets.

In a large bowl, sift together the flour, cocoa, baking soda, and salt. Set aside.

Bring 1 inch of water to a simmer in the bottom of a double boiler or a saucepan. Place the bittersweet chocolate in the top of the double boiler or in a heatproof bowl placed over the pan, and heat, stirring frequently, until the chocolate melts. Remove from the heat.

In a large bowl, using an electric mixer set on medium speed, cream together the 1 cup butter and brown sugar until smooth. Add the eggs one at a time, beating well after each addition. Add the melted chocolate and continue mixing until incorporated. Add the flour mixture in 2 batches and mix until a dough forms. Stir in the white chocolate morsels and walnut halves until evenly distributed.

Drop by tablespoons onto the prepared baking sheets. Bake until firm to the touch and beginning to crisp at the edges, about 10 minutes. Let cool on the baking sheets for 2 minutes, then, using a spatula, transfer the cookies to a wire rack. Serve warm, or let cool completely and store in a covered container at room temperature for up to 3 days.

Milk Chocolate–Dipped Macaroons ↔ makes 6 large cookies

Typically macaroons are small cookies made with almond paste or ground almonds, but these macaroons are different on two accounts. First, they are not small at all. Instead, they are made large so that they better retain moisture and texture. Second, they are made with coconut and receive a royal treatment—dipped in milk chocolate and drizzled with white chocolate. These macaroons are big, so grab a knife and share with a friend. —FARIS ZOMA

1 can (14 ounces) sweetened condensed milk

1 tablespoon pure vanilla extract

$1/2$ teaspoon kosher salt

4 cups (1 pound) sweetened shredded coconut

1 cup (6 ounces) milk chocolate morsels

2 teaspoons canola oil

$1/4$ cup white chocolate morsels

Preheat the oven to 350°F. Line the bottom of 2 rimmed baking sheets with parchment paper.

In a large bowl, stir together the sweetened condensed milk and vanilla. Stir in the salt and coconut and mix until thoroughly combined. Cover and chill the mixture in the refrigerator for about 1 hour to allow the coconut to absorb some of the liquid.

To form the cookies, use a 4-ounce, spring-action-grip ice-cream scoop. Pack the coconut mixture tightly into the scoop and release onto a prepared pan; repeat to form 6 portions. Bake the cookies, rotating the pan 180 degrees after 10 minutes to ensure even baking, until lightly browned, about 25 minutes. Remove from the oven, set the pan on a wire rack, and let the cookies cool completely on the pan.

Bring 1 inch of water to a simmer in the bottom of a double boiler or in a saucepan. Place the milk chocolate morsels and the canola oil in the top of the double boiler or in a heatproof bowl placed over the pan of water. Warm the chocolate, stirring frequently, until it melts. Remove from the heat.

Dip each cooled macaroon halfway into the melted chocolate and then set on the other prepared pan. Place the cookies in the refrigerator until the chocolate sets. Follow the same method to melt the white chocolate. Using the tines of a fork, drizzle white chocolate over the chocolate dipped portion of each cookie. Let the chocolate set before serving. Store in an airtight container at room temperature for up to 3 days.

Nonna's Traditional Biscotti

↔ makes 4 to 5 dozen cookies

This recipe was brought from Italy by my great-grandparents. During the holidays my **nonna** *always had an abundance of biscotti on hand for dipping into coffee or a glass of Merlot.* —ALLISON BARSOTTI

$1^1/_2$ cups (3 sticks) unsalted butter, at room
    temperature, plus more for preparing
    baking sheet

$1^1/_2$ cups sugar

5 large eggs

1 tablespoon anise extract

4 cups all-purpose flour, plus more for preparing
    baking sheet

4 teaspoons baking powder

$^1/_2$ teaspoon kosher salt

2 teaspoons aniseeds

1 cup chopped nuts, such as almonds or hazelnuts,
    or whole pine nuts

In a large bowl, using an electric mixer set on medium speed, cream together the $1^1/_2$ cups butter and sugar until light and fluffy. Beat in the eggs one at a time, beating well after each addition. Add the anise extract and beat until incorporated.

In a separate bowl, stir together the 4 cups flour, baking powder, and salt. With the mixer on low speed, add the dry ingredients 1 cup at a time, beating just until the flour disappears. Stir in the aniseeds and the nuts. Transfer the dough to a well-floured surface and knead until smooth, about 2 minutes. Let the dough rest for about 15 minutes.

While the dough is resting, preheat the oven to 325°F. Butter a baking sheet and then dust the sheet with flour, tapping out the excess.

Divide the dough into 3 equal parts. Using your palms, roll each portion back and forth on the floured work surface to form a log almost 1 inch in diameter. Arrange the logs on the prepared baking sheet, spreading them about 3 inches apart.

Bake the logs until lightly browned, about 15 minutes. Remove from the oven and let the logs cool for about 20 minutes.

Transfer the logs to a cutting board and, using a serrated knife, cut the logs on the diagonal into $^3/_4$-inch-thick slices. Return the slices, cut-side down, to the baking sheet (you may need 2 baking sheets to fit all the slices). Bake the slices, turning them over once, until they are dry, about 5 minutes. Remove from the oven and transfer to wire racks to cool. Store in an airtight container at room temperature for up to 3 days.

White Chocolate–Cherry Biscotti

↔ makes 4 to 5 dozen cookies

While many biscotti are dry, hard, and uninteresting, this version has a cookielike quality that people seem to love. The white chocolate plays well with the tart and sweet dried cherries, and the pistachios provide a nice textural counterpoint. Serve the biscotti with dessert wine or coffee for dipping. –JOHN BIRDSALL

$1/2$ cup (1 stick) ice-cold unsalted butter, cut into small cubes, plus more for preparing baking sheet

$1^3/4$ cups all-purpose flour, plus more for preparing baking sheet

$1/2$ cup sugar

1 teaspoon baking powder

$1/4$ teaspoon kosher salt

$3/4$ cup dried cherries

$1^1/4$ cups (about 7 ounces) white chocolate morsels

$3/4$ cup (about 3 ounces) shelled pistachios

2 large eggs

2 teaspoons pure vanilla extract

Preheat the oven to 350°F. Butter a baking sheet and then dust the sheet with flour, tapping out the excess.

In a food processor fitted with the metal blade, combine the $1^3/4$ cups flour, sugar, baking powder, and salt, and process until well mixed. Scatter the $1/2$ cup butter over the flour mixture and pulse about 20 times until the mixture resembles a damp, coarse meal. It should look like pie dough before it is gathered into a ball. Transfer the dough to a large bowl.

Add the cherries, chocolate, and pistachios to the dough and stir to combine. In a small bowl, whisk together the eggs and vanilla. Add to the flour mixture and stir to combine. Form the dough into a ball, cover, and refrigerate to relax the dough for 1 hour.

Divide the dough into 2 equal portions. Using your palms, roll each portion back and forth on the floured work surface to form a log about 2 inches in diameter. Arrange the logs on the prepared baking sheet, spacing them about 3 inches apart. Press the logs with your palms to flatten slightly.

Bake the logs until they are golden and beginning to crack on the top, about 30 minutes. Remove from the oven and let the logs cool for about 20 minutes. Reduce the oven temperature to 275°F.

Transfer the logs to a cutting board and, using a serrated knife, cut the logs on the diagonal into $3/4$-inch-thick slices. Return the slices, cut-side down, to the baking sheet (you may need 2 baking sheets to fit all the slices). Bake the slices, turning them over once, until they are dry, 15 to 18 minutes. Remove from the oven and transfer to wire racks to cool. Store in an airtight container at room temperature for up to 3 days.

Nanaimo Bars

↦ makes about 24 bars

This is one of those treats that reminds me of home and the holidays. I grew up in Alberta, Canada, where these bars are standard fare for the holidays. Audrey Sykes, a friend of mine from England, had an especially great recipe that she was kind enough to make for the Berkovich family. Here is the recipe. —YVONNE BERKOVICH

FIRST LAYER

$^1/_2$ cup (1 stick) unsalted butter, melted

$^1/_4$ cup firmly packed light brown sugar

2 tablespoons Dutch-processed cocoa powder

2 large egg whites, lightly beaten

2 cups graham cracker crumbs (about 25 crackers)

1 cup sweetened flaked coconut

$^1/_2$ cup chopped walnuts

SECOND LAYER

2 cups powdered sugar

4 tablespoons ($^1/_2$ stick) unsalted butter, at room temperature

$^1/_4$ cup heavy (whipping) cream

2 tablespoons custard powder (see Cook's Note)

THIRD LAYER

$^2/_3$ cup (4 ounces) semisweet chocolate morsels

4 tablespoons ($^1/_2$ stick) unsalted butter

First, prepare the baking dish. Line a 7-by-11-by-2-inch glass baking dish with 2 strips of parchment paper, each about 8 inches wide and 16 inches long. Let the excess overhang the sides, forming a sling for easy lifting and removal of the layered block from the dish once it is baked. Set aside.

To make the first layer, in a large bowl, combine the melted butter, brown sugar, cocoa powder, egg whites, cracker crumbs, coconut, and walnuts and mix thoroughly. Press firmly into the bottom of the prepared baking dish. Place in the freezer for 30 minutes.

To make the second layer, in a bowl, using a sturdy spoon, combine the powdered sugar, butter, cream, and custard powder, stirring until smooth and fluffy. The mixture will be fairly stiff. Spread evenly on top of the first layer. Place in the refrigerator while making the third layer.

To make the third layer, bring 1 inch of water to a simmer in the bottom of a double boiler or in a saucepan. Place the chocolate and butter in the top of the double boiler or in a heatproof bowl placed over the pan of water. Heat, stirring frequently, until the chocolate and butter melt. Using the back of a spoon, spread the warm chocolate topping evenly over the second layer and refrigerate until cold.

To serve, grasp the ends of the parchment and lift out the layered block from the dish. Using a sharp knife, cut into about 24 bars. Cover and refrigerate leftover bars for up to 3 days.

COOK'S NOTE: *Look for Bird's or Westco brand custard powder in well-stocked supermarkets or in specialty stores that carry baking and cake-decorating supplies.*

Renee's Lemon Bars

↦ makes about 18 bars

I have been baking these lemon bars for years, and my husband, who's a chef, borrowed the recipe to use in a restaurant where he was working. He once served them to The Fonz—the actor Henry Winkler. When my husband told The Fonz that it was my recipe, The Fonz instructed the chef to give me a big kiss for such a wonderful dessert. Now, everybody knows that you don't mess with The Fonz, so my husband passed the compliment along. –RENEE DUVALL-NORTHERN

CRUST

1 cup (2 sticks) unsalted butter,
    at room temperature, plus more for
    preparing baking pan
1 cup powdered sugar
2 cups all-purpose flour

FILLING

4 large eggs
2 cups granulated sugar
1 tablespoon grated lemon zest
6 tablespoons fresh lemon juice
$\frac{1}{3}$ cup all-purpose flour
1 teaspoon baking powder

Powdered sugar for dusting

To make the crust, preheat the oven to 325°F. Butter a 9-by-13-inch baking pan.

In a large bowl, using an electric mixer set on medium-low speed, cream together the 1 cup butter and powdered sugar until light and fluffy, stopping to scrape down the sides of the bowl once. Add the flour and mix until well blended. Spread the mixture in an even layer on the bottom and up the sides of the prepared pan.

Bake the crust until lightly browned, 15 to 20 minutes. Remove from the oven and set on a wire rack to cool completely. Raise the oven temperature to 350°F.

To make the filling, in a bowl, using an electric mixer set on medium-high speed, beat the eggs until well blended, about 2 minutes. Add the granulated sugar and beat until thick. Add the lemon zest, lemon juice, flour, and baking powder and beat until well blended and pale yellow. Pour the filling over the baked crust, and use a rubber spatula to spread it evenly.

Bake until the filling is set—firm on the edges, but still a little soft in the middle—15 to 20 minutes. Remove from the oven and set on a wire rack to cool slightly. Using a fine-mesh sieve or a sifter, dust the top with powdered sugar while still warm. Cut into bars about 3 by 2 inches and serve warm. Cover and store in the refrigerater for up to 3 days.

Neighborhood Brownies

↔ makes 16 brownies

I've used this brownie recipe for years. All of my mother's neighborhood friends exchanged their best recipes with one another and this was one of the recipes that always gets rave reviews. Experiment with using your own favorite extras: I am particularly fond of walnuts and lots of chocolate chunks, instead of morsels. Try one of the gourmet chocolates like Scharffen Berger or Valrhona, and chop the chocolate bars into miniature chunks. –GAIL LALUMIERE

Vegetable-oil cooking spray

$^3/_4$ cup (1$^1/_2$ sticks) unsalted butter

3 ounces unsweetened chocolate, finely chopped

1$^1/_2$ cups sugar

3 large eggs, lightly beaten

$^3/_4$ cup all-purpose flour

4 ounces good-quality semisweet chocolate,
    cut into $^1/_4$- to $^1/_2$-inch chunks

$^3/_4$ cup chopped walnuts, toasted (optional; see
    Cook's Note, page 190)

Preheat the oven to 350°F. Spray an 8-inch square baking pan with cooking spray.

In a saucepan over low heat, melt the butter and add the unsweetened chocolate. Stir until all the chocolate is melted and then remove from the heat.

Stir in the sugar and then let the mixture cool slightly. Add the eggs and stir to combine. Add the flour and stir to make a smooth batter. Add the chocolate chunks and stir to distribute evenly. If desired, add the toasted nuts at this point and stir until well combined. Pour the batter into the prepared pan, spreading it evenly with a rubber spatula.

Bake until a crust forms on top and the center is still somewhat gooey, 20 to 25 minutes. The brownies should be very fudgy and moist. It's better to underbake them than to overbake them. Remove from the oven and set on a wire rack to cool.

Cut into 2-inch squares to serve. Store in a covered container at room temperature up to 2 days.

KIDS' CAFÉ

Kids' Fried Rice

↔ serves 4

I haven't met a kid yet who doesn't love fried rice. This is a simple recipe with ingredients that are easily interchangeable to suit a variety of tastes. The secret to making fried rice that doesn't clump together is to use rice that has been cooked, cooled, and spread out to dry on a baking sheet in the refrigerator.

1 tablespoon canola oil

2 large eggs, lightly beaten

3/4 cup chopped, cooked chicken

2 slices ham, chopped

2 green onions, including green tops, chopped

1 cup frozen cut-up vegetables such as carrots or snow peas, or frozen whole peas, or a combination

2 1/2 cups cooked white rice, well dried (see recipe introduction)

2 tablespoons soy sauce

In a large skillet over medium-high heat, warm the oil and swirl to coat the bottom of the pan. Add the eggs and cook, stirring constantly, until cooked through. Scoot these off to one side of the pan and add the chicken, ham, green onions, and vegetables. Sauté, stirring constantly, until heated through, about 3 minutes. Scoot the eggs back in and then add the rice and soy sauce. Sauté, stirring and tossing, until the rice is heated through and all the ingredients are well combined. Serve immediately.

Simple Buttered Noodles

↔ serves 8

To most children, pasta is heavenly food, as long as you keep it simple. The maximum legal limit of ingredients that my son, Jarod, allows in what he used to call "macabonie" is four—pasta, salt, butter, and real Italian Parmesan cheese. Any more than these he considers a crime against pasta. Jarod knows his Parmesan cheese and likes the good stuff—Parmigiano-Reggiano.

1 tablespoon kosher salt, plus salt to taste

1 box (1 pound) pasta, a fun shape

3 tablespoons unsalted butter, at room temperature

Freshly grated Parmesan cheese, preferably
    Parmigiano-Reggiano

Fill an 8- to 10-quart stockpot two-thirds full of water and bring to a boil over high heat. Add 1 tablespoon salt to the boiling water and then add the pasta. Stir and cook the pasta until al dente (cooked through, but still slightly chewy), about 10 minutes.

Drain the pasta in a colander but do not rinse, and return it to the pasta cooking pot. Add the butter, toss to coat, and season with salt. Divide evenly among warmed bowls and sprinkle lots of cheese over the top. Serve immediately.

Kids' Campfire-Roasted Dinner

↔ *serves 8 campers*

This recipe is ideal for a camping trip with the kids. They can help assemble the packets before leaving, which can be the first meal of the camping adventure. The packets can be made and refrigerated up to 8 hours ahead. By having the kids involved in the preparation, they can customize their meals, selecting the vegetables they want to eat. Of course, the traditional dessert after this meal is toasted marshmallows or, better yet, campfire s'mores. –CHEF DAVID SHAW

1 chicken (3^1/$_2$ pounds), trimmed of excess fat
and cut into 8 pieces

16 baby new potatoes, halved

1 head garlic, separated into cloves and peeled

4 carrots, peeled and cut into big chunks

2 ears corn, shucked and each ear quartered
crosswise

2 large yellow onions, quartered through the
stem end

4 plum tomatoes, cored and halved lengthwise

^{1}/$_2$ cup olive oil

2 tablespoons fresh rosemary leaves, plus 8 sprigs

4 teaspoons kosher salt

2 teaspoons freshly ground black pepper

Place the chicken, potatoes, garlic, carrots, corn, onions, and tomatoes in a very large bowl. Drizzle with the olive oil, sprinkle with the rosemary leaves, and season with the salt and pepper. Cut 16 sheets of heavy-duty aluminum foil into 14-inch lengths. Lay 2 sheets of foil on a work surface, one on top of the other, to create a double thickness. On one half of the foil, place 1 piece of chicken. Arrange 4 potato pieces, 1 garlic clove, 2 carrot chunks, 1 piece of corn, 1 onion quarter, and 1 tomato half around the chicken. Garnish with a rosemary sprig. Fold the foil over the chicken and vegetables, and then roll, crimp, and seal the edges tightly to form a packet. Repeat to make 8 packets of chicken and vegetables. Refrigerate the packets until ready to cook.

Build a campfire and allow it to burn until you have some orange coals. Pull some of the coals away from the center of the fire to create a thin, even bed. Set the packets, top-side up, on the coals and scoot some additional coals around the packets. Cook the packets, replenishing the coals as needed, for 50 to 70 minutes. Open 1 packet to test for doneness; the chicken juices should run clear when the meat is pierced with a knife in the thickest part and the vegetables should be tender.

To serve, open the packets carefully and enjoy.

Christmas French Toast Strata

↔ serves 6 to 8

After a Christmas Eve filled with church going, gift giving, and celebration, I usually prepare this recipe. Friends and family who are spending the night help me put together the dish before they head for bed. On Christmas Day, I just turn on the oven and put the dish in to bake. –LORI SMITH

1 loaf French bread (1 pound),
   cut into 1-inch cubes (about 12 cups)

1 package (8 ounces) cream cheese,
   cut into small cubes

8 large eggs

$2^{1}/_{2}$ cups milk

6 tablespoons unsalted butter, melted, plus
   more for preparing baking dish

$^{1}/_{4}$ cup pure maple syrup, plus more for serving

1 small jar (about 8 ounces) of your favorite jam

Lightly butter a 9-by-13-inch baking dish. Scatter half of the bread in the bottom of the baking dish and arrange the cubes of cream cheese on top. Top with the remaining bread.

In a blender, combine the eggs, milk, 6 tablespoons butter, and $^{1}/_{4}$ cup maple syrup and process until well blended. Pour this mixture evenly over the bread and cream cheese in the pan. Using a spatula, lightly press the bread down to moisten it. Drop teaspoons of the jam over the top. Cover with plastic wrap and refrigerate overnight.

About 1 hour before serving, preheat the oven to 325°F. Remove the plastic wrap and place the dish in the oven. Bake until the center is set and the edges are golden brown, 35 to 40 minutes. Remove from the oven and set on a wire rack to set up and cool slightly, about 5 minutes. Serve with maple syrup.

Little Chefs'
Banana–Chocolate Chunk Bread → makes 2 loaves

My favorite "chef" team is Kelly and Tory Wilson, my six-year-old niece and eight-year-old nephew. They are creative, "hands-on" chefs who have developed new and unique ways to smash bananas and create chocolate chunks. This recipe for their special banana bread makes two loaves—plenty for family members who sneak into the kitchen late at night for a slice. –CHEF KIMBERLY SCHOR

$3/4$ cup ($1^1/2$ sticks) unsalted butter, at room temperature, plus more for preparing loaf pans

All-purpose flour for preparing loaf pans

$3^1/4$ cups cake flour

$1/2$ teaspoon baking soda

4 teaspoons baking powder

$1/4$ teaspoon kosher salt

$3/4$ cup ($1^1/2$ sticks) unsalted butter, at room temperature, plus more for preparing loaf pans

$1^1/3$ cups sugar

4 large eggs

3 cups mashed ripe bananas

$2/3$ cup sour cream

1 cup (6 ounces) semisweet chocolate chunks or morsels

Preheat the oven to 350°F. Butter two 9-by-5-by-3-inch loaf pans and then dust the pans with all-purpose flour, tapping out the excess.

In a large bowl, sift together the cake flour, baking soda, baking powder, and salt. Set aside.

In a large bowl, using an electric mixer set on medium speed, cream together the $3/4$ cup butter and sugar until light yellow and creamy. Add the eggs one at a time, beating well after each addition. Reduce the mixer speed to low and add the bananas and sour cream. Beat until incorporated. Add the flour mixture in 3 batches, beating after each addition just until the flour disappears. Using a rubber spatula, fold in the chocolate. Divide the batter evenly between the prepared pans.

Bake for 20 minutes, then rotate the pans 180 degrees. Continue to bake until a toothpick inserted near the center comes out clean, about 30 minutes longer. Remove from the oven and set on a wire rack to cool for at least 15 minutes before removing from the pan. Serve warm or at room temperature.

Birthday Fond Doo-4-U

↔ serves 8 to 10

At family gatherings, small children sometimes need a little space for themselves, a place to go off and make new friends and enjoy old ones. This is a tasty treat, easy to prepare, and incredibly fun for kids to eat. For my daughter Stephanie's fifth birthday, we set up a small separate table and let the children dip fruit and cake to their heart's delight.

1 cup hot fudge sauce

2 tablespoons water

$^1/_4$ cup chocolate-flavored syrup

2 pints strawberries, hulled

4 ripe bananas, peeled and each cut into 5 chunks

$^1/_4$ prepared angel food cake,
    cut into $1^1/_2$-inch cubes

20 marshmallows

In a small saucepan over medium-low heat, warm the fudge sauce, water, and chocolate syrup, stirring until well combined and smooth. Let cool slightly and then transfer to a dipping bowl. Place the dipping bowl in the center of a large platter and arrange the strawberries, banana chunks, cake cubes, and marshmallows around the bowl. (I use our Thanksgiving turkey platter and the children don't seem to mind!) Put one child in charge of the parents and other adults because they just might ravish more of the fondue than the children.

S'mores without the Campfire

↪ serves 4

Here is a quick and easy treat, and you won't have to worry about burnt marshmallows. This decadent dessert consists of only four ingredients, but your kids will think you are a culinary genius when it's served toasty brown and streaked with chocolate syrup.

4 graham cracker rectangles

2 milk chocolate bars (1^1/$_2$ ounces each), broken into sections

24 marshmallows

^{1}/$_4$ cup chocolate-flavored syrup

Preheat the oven to 375°F. Lay the graham crackers on an ungreased baking sheet. Place sections of the chocolate bars over the graham crackers. Top the chocolate evenly with the marshmallows.

Bake until the marshmallows are lightly puffed and perfectly toasted, about 7 minutes. Transfer to serving plates. Use a plastic squeeze bottle or the tines of a fork to streak thin diagonal lines of chocolate sauce across the toasted marshmallows. Eat while gooey and hot!

Chocolate–Cream Cheese Cupcake Comfort ↪ makes 12 cupcakes

This is my mother's cupcake recipe. My mom was a fantastic cook, with a huge repertoire of recipes. With three skinny boys to feed, she was always cooking, making certain we had enough to eat. Sometimes my brothers and I would come home from school and there would be a batch of these cupcakes set out on the table with three tall, cold glasses of milk. That's an after-school snack! –ERIK NORDSTROM

FILLING

1 package (8 ounces) cream cheese,
    at room temperature

$1/4$ cup sugar

1 large egg

$1/8$ teaspoon kosher salt

$1/2$ cup (3 ounces) semisweet chocolate morsels

BATTER

$1/2$ cup (3 ounces) semisweet chocolate morsels

$1^1/2$ cups all-purpose flour

$1/2$ cup sugar

1 teaspoon baking soda

$1/2$ teaspoon kosher salt

$1/2$ cup vegetable oil

1 large egg

1 teaspoon pure vanilla extract

1 cup water

Preheat the oven to 350°F. Line a standard-sized muffin pan with paper liners.

To make the filling, in a bowl, using a wooden spoon, mix together the cream cheese, sugar, egg, salt, and chocolate morsels until well blended. Set aside.

To make the batter, bring 1 inch of water to a boil in the bottom of a double boiler or in a saucepan. Place the chocolate morsels in the top of the double boiler or in a heatproof bowl placed over the pan. Heat, stirring frequently, until the chocolate is melted. Set aside to cool.

In another bowl, stir together the flour, sugar, baking soda, and salt. In a large bowl, whisk together the oil, egg, and vanilla. Stir in the melted chocolate. Add the flour mixture in 3 batches, alternating with the water, beginning and ending with the flour mixture and stirring until smooth. Spoon batter into each of the prepared muffin cups, filling them half full. Spoon about 2 tablespoons of the filling into each cup and top with the remaining batter.

Bake the cupcakes until they are puffed, slightly cracked on top, and baked through, 20 to 23 minutes. Remove from the oven and set on a wire rack to cool slightly. Serve warm.

Index

ACKNOWLEDGMENTS

This book may never have been written were it not for the support, encouragement, and direction provided by John Clem. Of special value was all of the behind-the-scenes assistance and the quality administrative efforts provided by Laurel Ewing. To Blake and Erik Nordstrom—thank you for understanding the potential of this work and for believing in me.

I was fortunate to have the assistance of Diane Morgan, a talented food writer and cookbook author in her own right. Thank you for all the hours spent in polishing and perfecting the recipes and ideas.

I have great appreciation for all of the support and efforts of Chef David Shaw, who helped bring this book from concept to reality. Thanks for the insight, the energy, and all of the work during the important task of carefully testing and adjusting each recipe.

I have long admired the world-class photography of E.J. Armstrong. Now, having had the opportunity to work with her, and with her team, I feel fortunate for the experience. E.J.'s strong passion for food and her artistic talents shine through in colorful jewel-like tones while clearly expressing the values and the intention of this work. The sense of vitality and family that E.J. kept alive during the photo sessions allowed the entire team to perform to their full potential.

The food styling of Patty Wittmann and Diana Isaiou deserves special recognition for all of their efforts and contributions to the photography in this work. Their beautiful food without trickery or sleight of hand makes these precious photographs real and inspiring.

To Gretchen Scoble, who created the design for this book, my gratitude. Thank you for weaving together a fabric that so finely supports the efforts of the many contributors by being true to expressing yourself through your art.

Thank you to Leslie Jonath, Lisa Campbell, and Sara Schneider at Chronicle Books for your patience, expert guidance, and wisdom throughout the evolution of this book. Although this is the first book that we have done together, it never once seemed like it due to the insightful direction that you each provided in turn.

Of course, none of this would have been possible without the ideas and recipes provided by the contributors to the book. Thank you all for providing food and inspiration that results in a work that is greater than the sum total of its parts.

A special thanks to all of my friends and family for providing inspiration, support, and those quiet moments of reflection that kept the goal of this work ever in focus.

—MICHAEL NORTHERN